Eric Nagler

MAKES MUSIC

30 MUSICAL INSTRUMENTS ANY FOOL CAN MAKE (EVEN ME)

A
Family
Activity
Book

ERIC NAGLER
and
Diana Buckley

McGRAW-HILL RYERSON LIMITED

Toronto   Montreal

ISBN 0-07-549777-8

1 2 3 4 5 6 7 8 9 AP 8 7 6 5 4 3 2 1 0 9

First Published in 1989 by
McGraw-Hill Ryerson Limited
330 Progress Avenue
Scarborough, Ontario, Canada M1P 2Z5

Care has been taken to trace the ownership of any copyright material contained in this text. The publishers welcome any information that will enable them to rectify, in subsequent editions, any incorrect or omitted reference or credit.

Canadian Cataloguing in Publication Data
Nagler, Eric
    Eric Nagler makes music

    ISBN 0-07-549777-8

    1. Musical instruments – Construction – Amateurs'
    manuals. I. Buckley, Diana. II. Title.

ML460.N34 1989   781.91'028   C89-094732-5

Photos: Pages 5; 25 top right and bottom; 31 bottom, middle, and top right; 47 top; 70 bottom; and 81 top, bottom, and middle courtesy Rodney C. Daw. Page 6 bottom courtesy Fred Phipps and the CBC Television Network. Pages 6 top; 7; and 31 top left courtesy Michael Courtney and Cambium Film & Video Productions. Pages 25 top left; 70 top; 71 top; and 81 bottom right courtesy Lynda Powell. Page 47 bottom Whitman Golden Ltd.

Jacket and Book Design by Hania Fil
Illustrations by Stephen MacEachern

Printed and bound in Canada

CONTENTS

ERIC

When I was very little I would bang on the piano.

My mother would say, "Eric, please. That is a delicate instrument."

My father would say, "Stop that racket!"

So I would wait until my parents went to work and then I would bang on the piano.

My grandmother would say, "Eric, play *The Tennessee Waltz*. It's my favourite song." I would bang a little slower. "That's beautiful," my grandmother would say.

When I got a little older I actually learned to pick out the melody of *The Tennessee Waltz*. I would ask my grandmother to hum it and I would pick out the notes. One day my mother heard me picking out the melody to *The Tennessee Waltz*.

"Eric, you have a natural talent," she said.

"That boy needs lessons," said my father. "Someday he'll thank us."

I did not want lessons. My friend Glenna took lessons and she had to stay in a lot while the other kids were out playing.

"Just take lessons for three months," said my mother, "and then if you don't like them you can stop."

So I took lessons for three months. The teacher would play the song and show me the notes but I didn't read them. Instead I learned the songs by listening to the teacher hum it or play it, the same as I used to listen to my grandmother.

"Don't look at your hands," the teacher would say. "Look at the notes." I learned to play the songs without looking at my hands but I did not learn to read the notes. After a while the music got too long for me to remember by ear, but I still could not read the notes, so things got very difficult. Luckily, three months was up and I quit.

"I did not think you'd remember about the three months," said my mother.

"I counted the days," I said.

When I got older I met a boy who played the saxophone. He let me play it. I learned to play *The Tennessee Waltz* in no time.

That evening at dinner I asked for a saxophone. My parents looked at each other, then at me.

My mother said, "The saxophone is not a valid instrument."

My father said, "Learn the clarinet instead. Someday you'll thank us."

The next day my father brought home a clarinet, and my mother brought home a teacher from the symphony orchestra.

"Read the notes," said the teacher. "That note is flat. Bite harder. That note is sharp. Bite softer." I did not like to read notes. I did not like to bite harder and softer, and he would not teach me *The Tennessee Waltz*. I quit.

When I got older I was at a party and somebody played a Charlie Mingus record. I fell in love with the bass. The next evening I asked for a bass.

"I want to play *The Haitian Fight Song* like Charlie Mingus," I said. My father and mother looked at each other, and then at me.

"The bass is very limiting," said my mother. "The notes are all too low."

"Take up the cello," said my father. "Someday you'll thank us."

The next day after school I didn't go home right away. I sat by myself for a while in some bushes in a vacant lot around the block. I got home late for dinner and there was a cello standing in the corner of the dining room. But they were angry at me for being late and forgot to talk about the cello. The next day it was gone.

One day when I was a little older I was up in my room. I was supposed to be doing my homework. I heard a strange sound coming from downstairs. I threw down my comic book and ran downstairs. It was my older brother's friend playing the banjo. The moment I heard the banjo, my heart opened right up and the banjo music jumped right inside.

That evening at dinner I didn't say anything about the banjo. But the next day I got an old broken-down banjo from my brother's friend. Then I got on my bike and visited my grandmother. She gave me $20 to help buy a banjo skin and some strings. I used a wooden venetian blind slat to fix the neck and some screws to fix the pegs. Every day I would come home from school and play the banjo.

When my mother came home from work she would say, "I've had a very difficult day, dear."

My father would say, "Stop that racket."

I would go up to my room and play as quietly as I could. But banjoes are loud. My parents would yell at me from downstairs. I would go up to the furthest room in the attic, stuff an old pair of socks in my banjo, and continue to play.

Eventually my parents finished the basement in knotty pine, moved the old sofa and the TV down there, and for three years while I learned the banjo there was a sort of no-man's-land on the first and second floor of the house. Occasionally I would meet my parents on the stairs and they would ask me how my school work was coming.

"Fine," I would say. But my school work was not exactly fine. My heart was too filled with banjo music for me to concentrate very well on biology. And even though I promised my parents I would try, I never did become a doctor.

Instead, when I grew up I became a banjo player and made many people happy. My parents were very proud.

"That's my boy!" said my father.

"I always said he had a natural talent," said my mother.

ANY FOOL CAN DO IT

If I can do it, any fool can do it. Well, not exactly. Some fools can do it better than others. But it doesn't matter, you don't have to be a television or radio star to make music. We can all do it together and have lots of fun. After all, people have been playing and singing in family and community since before history...

...that is until TV came along. Now-a-days we're inclined to spend more time watching than doing. TV is such a powerful medium, it tends to isolate us from each other. But not so long ago, before the advent of the "boob tube," families and communities would gather regularly to make their own music.

And you know what? We miss it. We miss the action and the fun of joining in. I know, because at my concerts everybody wants to get into the act. And that's actually the whole idea behind these home-made instruments. It doesn't take 15 years of musical training to join in with a pair of spoons.

WHY MAKE MUSIC?

Music is a terrific way of expressing yourself. By making music it's possible to laugh and cry, tell a story, or paint a picture. Music helps you communicate who you are inside and get back the same from others.

Music also helps fit us into the framework of the people around us. When you make your own unique sound in harmony or together with the unique sounds of your buddies, music lets you be yourself and also feel connected to the group. Making music together becomes a very special experience of community.

YOUR BODY IS AN INSTRUMENT

Some people think that the only "real" instruments are the ancient ones for which classical music has been written. But an instrument can be anything. Our body is an instrument when we sing or dance, clap, whistle, snap, stomp, etc. Pick up a Bobby McFerrin tape and listen to him play *Thinkin' About Your Body*. He does all the musical parts by singing and slapping his body.

Put a kazoo in your mouth and your voice becomes quite different. Learn to play the fiddle and your fingers can express themselves in even more ways. Think of a musical instrument is an extension of your body. And don't forget that the music comes from inside you. The instrument is only there to help you get it out.

EASY ONES AND HARD ONES

At my concerts I teach people how to play the spoons, the comb kazoo, the jew's harp, an assortment of rattles and drums, etc. It takes just a few seconds to learn how to hold and manipulate these instruments and you can then use your natural body rhythm to make music. In just a short time the entire audience becomes an orchestra of clappers, key players, etc., and it sounds great!

For many of us, making music is such a good feeling that we want to go further. I like to play the banjo and fiddle, but you can't learn to make music on these instruments in a few short minutes. It's up to you to decide if you want to take the time to learn one of these. Whatever instrument you choose doesn't necessarily make the music better. It's all just different ways of expressing yourself.

THIS IS A BOOK ABOUT HOME-MADE INSTRUMENTS

You can spend as little or as much of your time and money as you like. You can use your body, or for nothing at all you can make your own instruments out of things that you can find around the house. In this book I'll show you how to make some great home-made instruments and tell you about other books that are available for the home-made instrument enthusiast.

THIS IS ALSO A BOOK ABOUT TRADITION

"Tradition" means something passed down from the past.

Music is as old as humanity, maybe even older. No one knows exactly how or when people first started making it. Musical traditions are transmitted from the past through songs, tunes, instruments, etc.

I find that by opening myself up to music from the past, I enter a kind of time machine that enables me to experience the ways people acted and felt long ago. If the songs are from my own tradition, why then it's like visiting my ancestors and learning a lot about who I am and where I came from. For a boy from the big city such as myself, learning the songs from a simpler rural life and time was quite an enlightenment.

Many people made music with my fiddle before I got it. I don't know if people actually leave a little part of themselves behind in their instruments, but my fiddle seems to have a spirit of its own when I'm making music with it. Who knows, maybe a hundred years from now some kid is going to find a kazoo in a junk shop. He'll put it to his lips and amazingly find himself humming *Come On In! Ain't Nobody Here But Me*.

It's tradition that gives me the ideas for my home-made instruments. They always start with an idea that I got from someone else. In this book I'll tell you about some of the people that taught me about music.

When I was growing up I often made music with my friends. We didn't just watch it or listen to it but we also made it. It was great. We used music to communicate with each other in the magical way that only music can. To me, that's what "folk music" means: people playing their music together. I learned a lot about musical tradition and became part of a musical community.

TRADE IN YOUR POPCORN FOR A PAIR OF SPOONS!

TV shows only the world's very best entertainers, which can be discouraging. We think, "Gee, I could never be that good so what's the use of trying?" But music isn't made by radios or televisions. It's made by people. And if you think listening to music is fun, you'll be surprised at how much better it is when you do it yourself! Like the song says:

> *It don't take no talent to do your part.*
> *Just as long as what you're doin' comes from the heart.*

So don't just sit there listening to music and eating popcorn. Get up, get together with some friends, put together some home-made instruments and make music! It's all a wonderful way of sharing yourself with others and of course letting others share themselves with you.

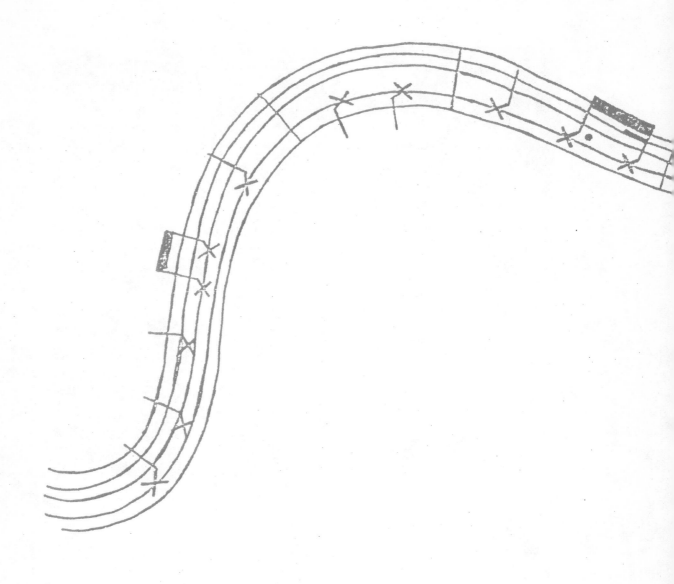

RHYTHM AND PERCUSSION

The stars at night
Are shining bright.
Clap clap clap clap clap.
Deep in the heart of Texas.

Some people are discouraged to find they can't keep a beat. I believe each of us is born with "natural" rhythm but it often gets trained out of us as we grow up. While Baby is in the womb it is bombarded not just by the beating of Mommy's heart but also her blood flowing, breathing, burping, talking, singing, and all the other activities of her body, which create a symphony of rhythm and music. It's loud in there! Tape recordings of inside the womb sound like a factory. By the time Baby pops out she's ready to bop. She just needs to put a little meat on her bones before she can boogie!

But as we grow up we're taught to use our heads and solve problems rationally... to place controls on our bodies and feelings. Unfortunately, heads aren't very good at rhythm. Music and rhythm are expressions of the whole body acting in regular motion, and when our mind tries to be the leader, rhythm breaks down. If you want to re-discover your natural rhythm, ask your head to take a back seat and let your body lead the way. It's not easy, but it is a learnable process.

When I was a kid, on a hot summer's afternoon I'd often join a bunch of friends gathered around a front stoop to bang out rhythms on garbage cans, iron railings, and boxes. It was lots of fun. At first I played quietly. As I got better I played a bit louder. I didn't know I was learning to play "percussion instruments," which is a big name for anything you hit, rub, shake, whirl, or scrape. Bells, shakers, rattles, and spoons are percussion instruments; so are drums and tin can bongos. Certain things that make noise when you hit or shake them should not be used as percussion instruments, such as younger siblings, pets, or heirloom china.

I use a lot of percussion instruments in concert because it takes only a few moments for people to learn, and you can use almost anything. In the song *My Dog Treed Rabbit* on the album *Fiddle Up a Tune*, we used congas, knee slaps, cowbells, a cardboard box, an ashtray, and hand claps. Make a rhythm instrument for yourself simply by finding something neat around the house to bang on.

SIMPLE SHAKERS

Many simple shakers can be made from "garbage." Here are some that I use in my concerts:

PLAY IT DON'T SLAY IT!!

The idea is not to be louder than everybody else, but to blend in. Try to pay as much attention to listening as to playing. Your turn to shine will come during your solo.

THE JUNK DRAWER SHAKER

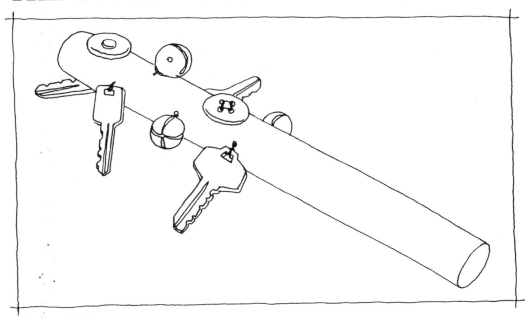

YOU NEED:

— 1 piece of 1" dowelling about 1' long. A piece of an old broom stick is
  perfect.
— A bunch of junk drawer goodies (keys, buttons, rings, bells or any-
  thing that makes a sound)
— String, such as fishing line, nylon string, or heavy cotton. I use bell
  wire because my shakers are played so heavily.
— A drill
— Sand paper
— A clamp

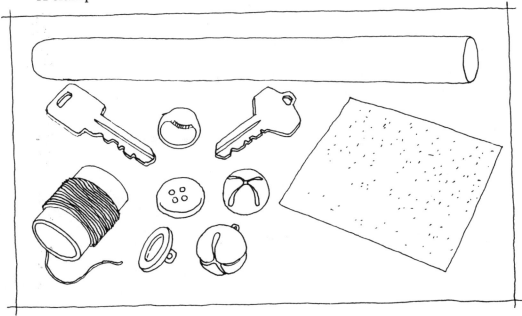

HERE'S WHAT TO DO:

Drill holes as shown in the diagram. An electric drill requires adult supervision. Clamping the dowel to a work bench keeps you from making holes in the kitchen floor... like I did... once.

Sand any rough edges. Cut four pieces of wire or string 1' long and attach buttons and junk to the dowelling.

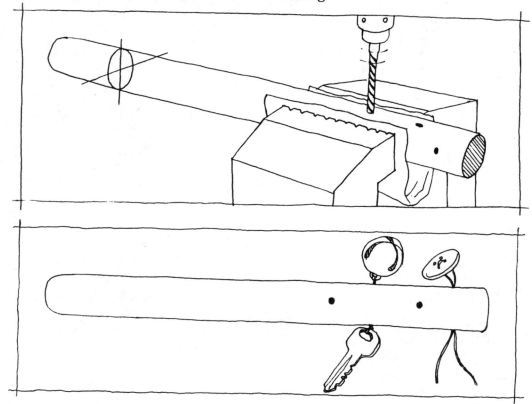

VARIATION:

An interesting variation to the junk drawer shaker is the dooley stick. To make it, use the entire broom stick instead of just a piece. Play the dooley stick by banging it on the floor.

THE PLASTIC BOTTLE CALABASH

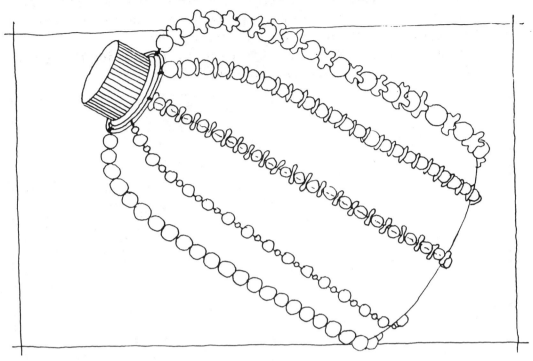

YOU NEED:

— 2 one-inch rings (macramé rings from a craft store work well)
— 1 plastic shampoo bottle
— An assortment of beads
— Nylon cord or wire
— Scissors
— Duct tape

HERE'S WHAT TO DO:

Cut eight lengths of string, each about 1 1/2 times the height of the bottle in length and tie them to the ring as in the diagram. Use tape to keep the ring centred to the bottom of the bottle.

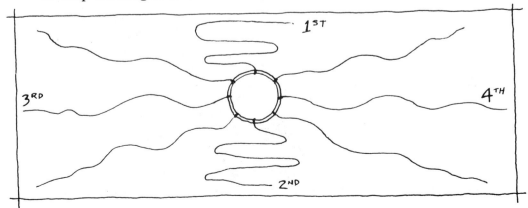

String the beads and tie the strings to the top ring. Trim off the excess string, remove the tape, and "voila"!

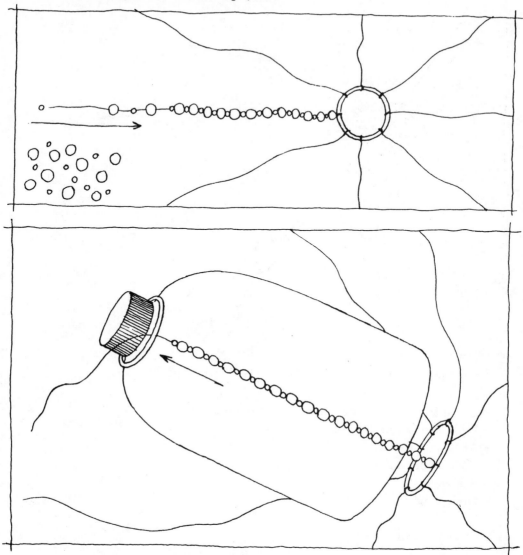

The calabash is a little easier to play if you push a dowel through the mouth of the bottle to make a handle. Secure the dowel with duct tape.

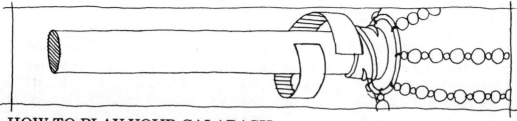

HOW TO PLAY YOUR CALABASH:

The calabash can be shaken, hit against your hand, or tossed and caught in rhythm to music.

THE GAZERNOWICH

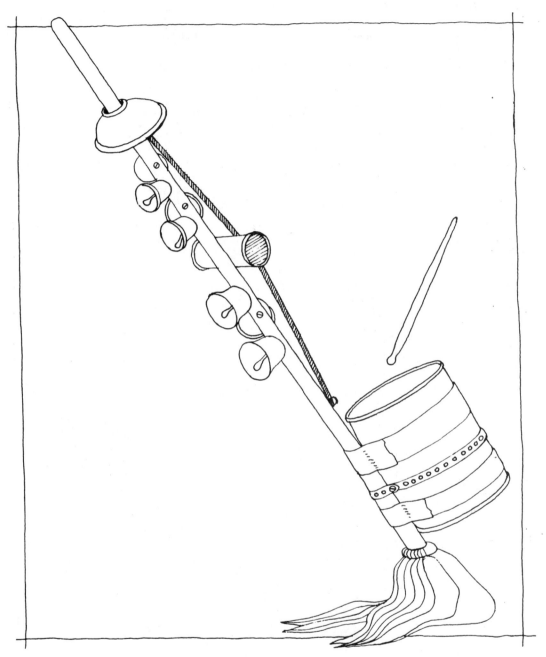

Several winters ago I flew with a theatre company to tiny communities in Northern Ontario. Many of them had no television and so the evenings were often filled with people making their own music. At one such gathering I first saw a fancy variation of the dooley stick, played by a woman who didn't know what to call it, so I dubbed it a gazernowich. It was made from an old mop, a spring, and a couple of large tin cans. She banged it on the floor, which added a great percussion section to the music. I made one similar to hers, but added bells for more variety. Here's how I made it:

YOU NEED:

— An old floor mop, a strong one about an inch thick
— A door spring
— A pop or soup can
— A large juice can or restaurant size can, one end removed
— 3 stove bolts and nuts at least 1 1/2" long
— 3 washers for the bolts
— A metal tightening band long enough to attach the can to the mop handle with a little overlap.
— A small nut and bolt (or duct tape)
— A stick to play the instrument with
— The rubber part of a toilet plunger or the top from a bleach bottle
— An assortment of bells and screws

TOOLS:

— A utility knife (to cut the toilet plunger or bleach bottle)
— A drill and small bit (to start holes for screws)
— A screw driver

HERE'S WHAT TO DO:

The gazernowich is made, in a similar manner to the junk drawer shaker, by drilling holes various points along the mop handle and attaching springs, bells, or cans to the stick with stove bolts. Be careful though. I weakened my first one by drilling too many holes too close together and it broke shortly after I installed the door spring.

Duct tape or a metal plumbing band will secure the large can attached near the base of the pole.

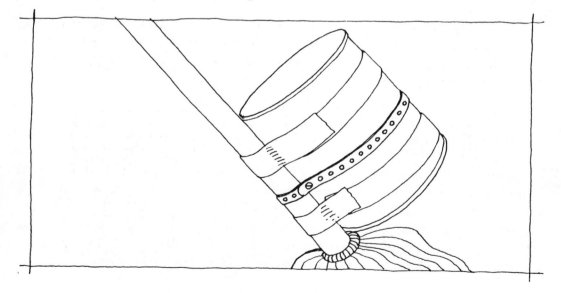

I needed a friend to stretch the spring along the mop handle while I attached it with a stove bolt. The spring exerts a lot of pressure and that's why you need a strong mop handle.

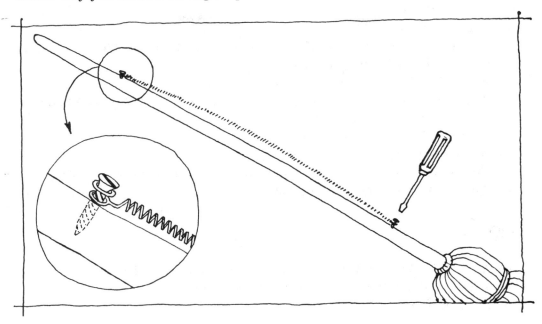

A cut section of bleach bottle (or toilet plunger, if you want to be fancy) slipped over the top will keep your hands from hitting the spring when you play.

HOW TO PLAY YOUR GAZERNOWICH:

If you are a righty, hold the mop in your left hand, the stick in your right. Bounce the mop on the floor and brush the stick along the spring on the up-bounce. For variety, hit the top of the tin can with the stick. I put tape all over the can top to deaden the volume. Try playing melodies on the bells.

Here are some rhythms I use. Have fun and make up some of your own. Be careful. In the hands of a rookie this instrument can have a devastating affect on parental emotional health. Play quietly except when soloing.... And don't solo that often!

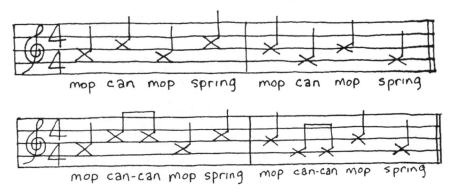

THE SPOONS

The spoons are one of my favourites: accessible, easy to play and get good at. But spoons can be very loud and percussive, so be attentive. If the people around you are holding their ears and making gruesome faces you may be playing too loud. Also, some tunes do not particularly lend themselves to spoons... *Plaisir D'amour*, for example.

I use a matching pair of round soup spoons... NOT MY MOM'S BEST SILVER. Crummy spoons usually sound better anyway. Smaller spoons work better for smaller hands.

Test out several until you get a pair that sounds good to you. I put duct tape on the inside of the bowls of my spoons so they make a "clunk" rather than a "clank." I also tape the ends of each spoon so they are less likely to fly out of my hand. I don't tape the spoons together though. Spoons attached at the ends of the handles are less versatile. I do put tape on the handle of the bottom spoon — the one which goes between my first and second finger — so that the metal doesn't dig into my skin. I also bend the top and bottom spoons differently so they fit my hand comfortably and the bowls strike in the centre.

To play the spoons, put them back to back and grab the handles with your index finger inbetween, separating the bowls as in the picture. **Hold them rather tightly so they don't flop around**. Hit your knee with the spoons so that the top one bangs against the bottom one. When you have a good rhythm and the spoons are not flopping all over the place, try holding your other hand above them and hit it on the upswing. Hitting your upper hand every other time gives a basic "Lone Ranger" rhythm. You know... "Where did the Lone Ranger take the garbage?" "To the dump... to the dump... to the dump, dump, dump."

Advanced spoonists can try the "brush." Spread your fingers out stiff, run the bottom spoon across the fingers and onto your knee. It makes a drum roll effect as you first hear when the spoons are played in *Momma Don't Low* on my *Fiddle Up a Tune* album.

Spoons are great percussion instruments to accompany your own songs. On the album *Come On In*, listen to *Spoons Tunes* which I put together from school yard rhymes and old verses. Make up your own "rap" for your own spoon tune.

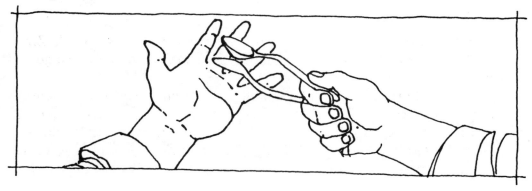

THE WASHBOARD

Washboards are not too common in hardware stores these days but I still see them fairly regularly in junk shops, garage sales, and flea markets. In fact, a lot of home-made instrument stuff is not too common these days. Things made of metal, wood, or cotton seem to sound better than their modern plastic offspring. It's unfortunate, but in another way that's what makes the searching more fun. Junk shops, flea markets, and the places where old things hang out become the fertile hunting grounds for instrument parts.

Washboard Hank is the best washboard player I know. He has so many gadgets, bells, noise makers, and doo-dads attached to his instrument that it weighs a ton. He wears a hard hat with a bell and pie plate attached just for added effect.

Watching him is as much fun as listening. Hank holds the instrument with his left hand, whipping his right around the board and his head with lightning speed, beating out tunes as well as rhythms.

YOU NEED:

— A metal washboard. The heavier the metal, the fuller the sound. Zinc is more durable than tin or aluminum. National Washboard is a good brand.
— A variety of attachments. Use any of the following or dream up some of your own: cowbells, woodblocks, pots, pans, bells, bike horns, a wok or pot lid for a cymbal. A lot of the fun in building this instrument is searching for bells and things that make specific notes so that you can work melodies into the rhythms.

— A variety of wood screws, clamps, wire, etc. to attach the noise makers to the instrument
— A cotton work glove (right if you're right handed)
— 4 metal thimbles
— Screw drivers
— Scissors
— Duct tape or heavy fabric tape

HERE'S WHAT TO DO:

Attach your noise makers to the washboard with screws, etc. If you're right handed, put the bells on the right side of the instrument as it's facing you, and vice-versa if you're a lefty. That way they will be convenient to reach. Also make sure you leave space to hold the instrument.

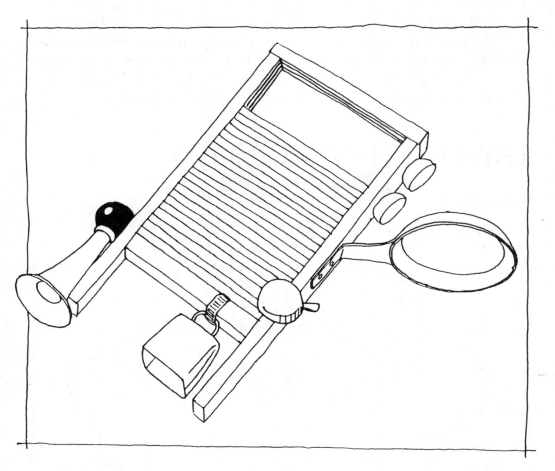

I play my washboard with a glove that has thimbles attached to the fingers. It sounds neat and saves my fingers. To make the glove, cut a hole in each of the four fingers of a glove (not the thumb). Leave the holes small so the thimbles fit in tight. Push the thimbles through the holes from inside the glove so that just the metal ends stick out, and tape them in place with duct tape.

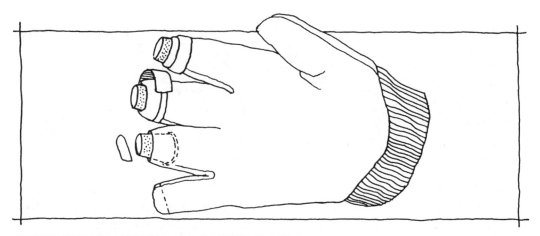

HOW TO PLAY YOUR WASHBOARD:

If you haven't made a thimble glove, you can use a pair of spoons, an old ring, thick wire, nail, stick, etc. Righties put the glove on the right hand and hold the washboard with the left. You can hold the board against your body or lay it on your lap. Rub and tap the metal ridges and the wooden frame and add the bells and other noise makers for variety. You can hear the washboard played on *Boom Boom Ain't It Great To Be Crazy* on the *Fiddle Up A Tune* album.

THE SIMPLE WASHBOARD

YOU NEED:

— A metal paint tray
— A wooden spoon

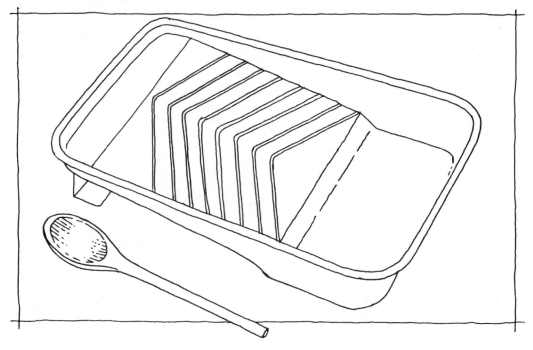

MY FIRST PERFORMANCE

My first official performance was a riot. My friends David Cohen, Arty Traum, and I formed a bluegrass group. A couple of times a week we'd get together and work up songs like *Rollin In My Sweet Baby's Arms, I Dipped In the Sugar Bowl — And All I Got Was Lumps, There'll Be No Detours In Heaven*... stuff like that. Of course we'd be at Washington Square without fail every Sunday. One day a man introduced himself as the program director of a park in lower Manhattan and asked if we'd like to do a forty-five minute set for him the following Saturday... and for money too: forty-five dollars! Gosh, that was fifteen bucks a piece. Through the week we practised up, made sure we had enough material, waited for Saturday afternoon, and headed for Manhattan.

In the park there was a concrete stage and rows of concrete benches. Figuring eight or nine to a bench, there was room for over two hundred people. Well, there were maybe thirty people scattered toward the back, and not including a few sleeping drunks the age ranged from about seventy-eight years old to ninety-five. There was something about the way they were dressed which suggested that they had not been born on this continent, and probably never heard a bluegrass tune in their lives.

"Didn't I tell you?" said the program director. "We're directly across the street from an old folks home. That's your audience."

What the heck. A gig's a gig. So we started off with *Rollin In My Sweet Baby's Arms* a fast tune with nice harmonies and lyrics you can relate to:

> *Where was you last Friday night*
> *While I was lyin in jail*
> *Walkin the streets with another man*
> *Wouldn't even go my bail.*
>
> *Rollin' in my sweet baby's arms*
> *Rollin' in my sweet baby's arms*
> *Lay around the shack till the mail train come back*
> *And I'm rollin' in my sweet baby's arms.*

When we finished there was no applause. There was no sound. No movement of any kind. Discarded crumpled papers did not rustle in the windless air.

Trees did not bend. David, Arty, and I looked at each other. Little beads of sweat began to form on David's forehead. We decided to do an even faster tune in the hopes of getting their attention:

There's a rabbit on a log and I ain't got my dog
How will I get him I know (woof woof)
I'll fetch me a briar and I'll twist it in his hair
And that way I'll get him I know (woof woof)

You've heard the expression, "oil painting"? This was a study in stone: Washington, Lincoln, Jefferson.... The sweat flowed freely on all three of us now. We discarded our prepared set list and decided to do no slow songs at all, fearing that it might slow someone's heart to a stop. We ripped through every fast number we knew. We jumped around, talking louder and louder between songs. Each tune burst forth with a more frenzied urgency than the last.

The drunks slept. The old folks sat. Not sat. Sat isn't the proper word. Because even when you sit something moves, some little thing. An eye blinks, a muscle twitches. Perhaps a fly is flicked off the face.... Nothing. When the forty-five minutes of Coventry was finally over and our torture concluded, we slunk off the stage with our shoulders bent, our egos dragging.

At that moment the program director came running up, his eyes bright, his face gleaming.

"DID YOU SEE THAT!!" he shouted. "DID YOU SEE THAT? I've never seen them like that before. You guys were incredible. You really had 'em goin'. Can you come back next week?"

David, Arty, and I looked at each other. The guy was obviously sincere. Apparently his experienced eye had observed some movement otherwise invisible. And what's more, we had apparently impressed this audience as no other group had all summer. WE WERE A HIT!!

What happened to David and Arty? Oh, they got over our initial trauma and went on to make their fortunes in music... and me? Well, among other things I'm writing this book...

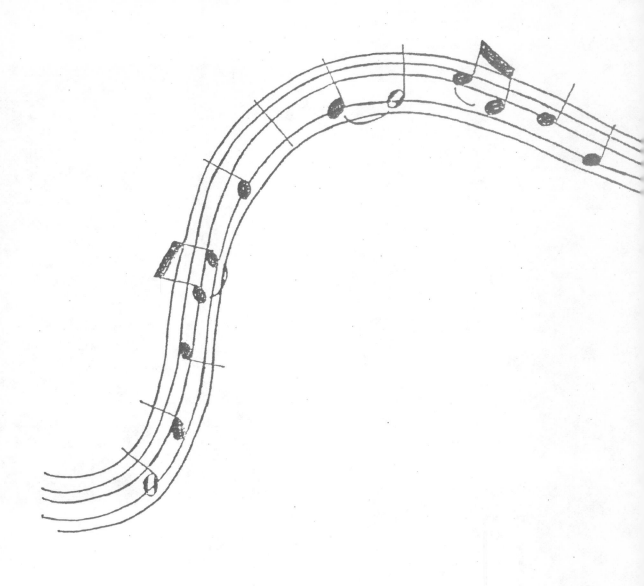

MORE ABOUT SOUND

Creating a musical instrument can be more fun if we know more about sound. Here are some basics.

SOUND

Sound happens when vibrating air hits our ear. Vibrating means shaking back and forth or up and down really fast. The vibrating thing makes the air around it vibrate. The vibrating air hits our ear and is experienced as sound. In other words, sound is vibrating air that hits your ear... unless you are a fish. If you're a fish, then it's water that is vibrating and hits your ear (fish have ears?) But never mind, the point is that water will transfer vibrations too. You can hear things under water, but there is no sound in a vacuum. Outer space is a vacuum, so when you hear spaceships go buzzing by in cheap science-fiction movies, they're wrong. I hate that.

TRY THIS:

Let's do a vibration experiment. Break a rubber band and stretch it between your foot and your hand. Pluck it.

What you see is the rubber band vibrating back and forth. You might hear something too. That's because the vibrations of the rubber band make a little bit of the surrounding air vibrate, and some of it reaches your ear. If you could see the air you would see it vibrating in waves like when a pebble drops into a pool of water. Let's check out vibration another way.

TRY THIS:

Take a thin, flexible piece of wood or metal like a ruler (either metric or imperial, doesn't matter) and hold it flat to a table or desk with the heel of your hand. Leave a good portion of the ruler overhanging. Pull this end down and let go.

What happens? Can you see the ruler vibrate?

INSTRUMENT MAKING RULE #1: **In order to make sound you have to get something to vibrate.** For example you could:

Pluck a string made of metal or nylon.
Hit the string with a mallet.
Bang on a metal tube.
Buzz your lips to make a Bronx Cheer.
Blow across the opening of a pop bottle top.
Hit a cookie sheet, or a wooden board, or a stretched animal skin.

These are all ways of creating vibrations... creating sound. The essence of sound is vibration.

TRY THIS:

Look around you. Which things will vibrate and which won't? Will your pillow vibrate? A leaf? A blob of jello?

Some things won't vibrate very well because they're too soft and squishy. Others are too delicate.

Only **stiff** things vibrate. A rubber band is stiff when you stretch it. A metal ruler is stiff. A thick board of wood is stiff too, but it is hard to make vibrate. If something is really big and thick like a church bell, it has to be hit very hard to make it vibrate. Rubber bands, on the other hand, have to be plucked very gently.

TRY THIS:

Look at some musical instruments and determine what parts are vibrating. What is vibrating on a drum, a piano, a saxophone, a violin, a bell, a trumpet?

AMPLIFICATION

Amplification means loudness. **The more air that vibrates the louder the sound**. Go back to that vibrating rubber band. It's not very loud because not very much air is vibrating.

TRY THIS:

Tie something small like a small screw to one end of a rubber band and thread the rubber band through the bottom of a paper cup from the inside so that the rubber sticks out the bottom. Tie this end to anything, even your toe. Pluck the stiff rubber band and listen into the cup.

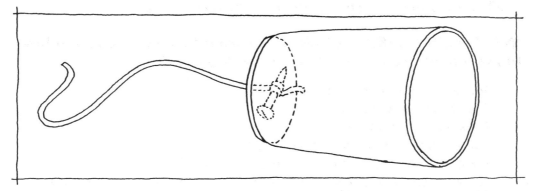

Now you should hear the sound pretty well. That's because the rubber band transfers vibrations to the bottom of the cup, which is a bigger vibrating surface. And the walls of the cup channel most of those vibrations right to your ear.

SOUND FROM STRINGS

Hey! Wadda ya know? I think we just made our first stringed instrument. The rubber band (the vibrator) is called a "string" and the paper cup is called a "resonator" because it resonates (makes louder) the sound. We could call our instrument a "rubber band harp" because, like a harp, the string attaches directly to the resonator and is not connected by a bridge. Or, we could call it a miniature washtub bass (see pages 41- 43)

INSTRUMENT MAKING RULE # 2: **A resonator makes the sound louder**. But remember that when you're inventing a musical instrument the vibrator has to match the resonator. Don't expect a rubber band to make a thick piece of wood vibrate and don't try vibrating a cardboard box with a heavy rope. I often see that kind of mistake in the home-made instruments people show me.
    Now let's talk about pitch.

PITCH

Pitch refers to whether the notes sound high or low. **If you make the vibrations happen faster or slower, the pitch will be higher or lower**.

TRY THIS:

Pluck your new rubber band harp while stretching the rubber band tighter and looser.

When you stretch it tighter the vibrations get faster and the sound goes higher. If you make the rubber band short by grabbing it closer to the cup, it will also sound higher for the same reason.

INSTRUMENT MAKING RULE # 3: **Tighter or shorter is higher. Looser or longer is lower**. It's the same principle with any kind of instrument. A longer (or looser) rubber band makes a lower sound. So does a longer tube, a bigger (or looser) drum, etc.

TRY THIS:

Look at different musical instruments again. Identify what is vibrating and what is resonating. Can the pitch be changed? And if so, how?

So these are the most important rules for making a musical instrument: Something has to vibrate. The more air vibrating the louder the sound will be. And to make the sounds higher and lower the speed of the vibrations has to vary.

Let's make some more stringed instruments.

THE BANJO WAS ONCE A HOME-MADE INSTRUMENT TOO!

Joel Sweeney, a farmer from Virginia is often credited with inventing the first five-string banjo (the kind I play). After a long day's work on the family farm, Joel liked to relax and make music with the slave workers. He would play fiddle and the workers played instruments that they'd made. One of them was probably a banjar, an instrument of African origin made by hollowing out a large gourd, stretching dried animal skin over the opening, attaching a wooden neck, and fitting it with a few strings.

   Joel modified his instrument by fitting a neck to a cheese box and adding a drone string. That's a string that stops half way up the neck and is not fingered, thus making the constant droning sound that is so characteristic of today's folk-style banjo. Joel began playing his home-made banjo in a band with his two brothers. As the band gained popularity so did the banjo and before long, several American instrument companies were making copies of Joel's home-made instrument.

   Although many people bought the manufactured instrument, some continued to design their own banjos. In a book called *Musical Instruments of the Southern Appalachian Mountains* there is an excellent collection of pictures of many home-made banjos. Each one is different. There's even one made from an old cake pan! I have a home made banjo that's made from a pressure cooker. It takes a few hours to make a banjo from a bleach bottle. Read on...

THE BLEACH BOTTLE BANJO

My friend Rick Avery first showed me a bleach bottle banjo. By the way, if you get a chance to hear him and his wife, Judy, perform you're in for a treat. I modified Rick's design to make a more substantial and louder banjo from a peanut butter pail. His is easier to make so I'll describe it first.

YOU NEED:

— A bleach bottle or any plastic bottle, the bigger the better. Get one with a flat bottom.
— 2 pieces of 1" x 3" wood for the neck. A broken hockey stick works, but soft wood like pine or spruce is much easier to carve and drill. The length should be about twice as long as the diametre of the bleach bottle.
— Nylon fishing line or a set of nylon banjo strings.
— 5 medium-sized wood screw eyes.
— 5 small nails or brads
— 1 small round-head slotted wood screw.
— A piece of wood about 2 1/2" x 1/2" x 1/4" for the bridge. The bridge is critical because it transfers the string vibrations to the banjo head. If the bridge is too thick the sound will be absorbed and muffled. So I cheated and spent $2.50 for a good quality five-string banjo bridge.
— A piece of wood for the nut, the width of the neck by 1/8" by 1/4". (A piece of a thin wooden ruler will do.)

TOOLS:

— A hammer
— A saw
— A utility knife
— A thin triangular file
— Sand paper
— A pocket knife
— Wood glue
— A surform plane

HERE'S WHAT TO DO:

With the utility knife cut the bleach bottle about 3" from the bottom. An adult should help with this part. Discard the top. The bottom turned upside down is your banjo head and skin.

Glue the two pieces of neck wood together as in the diagram. They overlap so that the bottom piece sticks out about 1" PLUS the diametre of the banjo head. This bottom piece is the post, and the top piece is the neck and fingerboard. If you wish, you can use the plane to shape the neck so it more closely resembles a "real" banjo neck.

Cut holes in the banjo head to stick the post through. The holes should be the same size or slightly smaller than the post, so it fits snugly. The placement of the holes will determine how high the strings will be from the fingerboard, and therefore how difficult the banjo will be to play. Take a look at the diagram. If the neck is 1" thick, then the top of hole #1 should be 1" from the skin. Hole #2 should be about 1/8" closer to the skin. This will make the fingerboard flush with the skin, and angled back slightly.

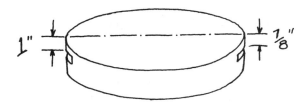

Use a thin file or saw to make a slot across the fingerboard about 4" from the end. It should be wide enough to snugly fit the nut. (Remember, your nut is about 1/8" wide)

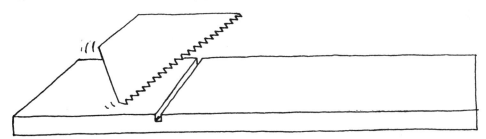

Glue the nut into its slot. When the glue is dry, file four notches in the nut equal distance apart for the strings to rest in.

Screw two screw eyes into each side of the fingerboard beyond the nut.

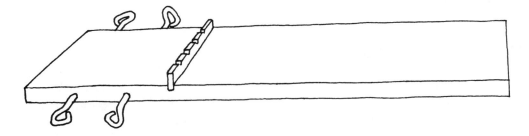

OPTIONAL: For a five-string banjo (the kind I play), place the fifth screw eye half way along the neck as shown. For the fifth string nut, screw in the small round- headed slotted screw as shown. The fifth string sits in the slot of the screw. If you are going to play the banjo lefty, place the fifth string nut on the opposite side of the neck.

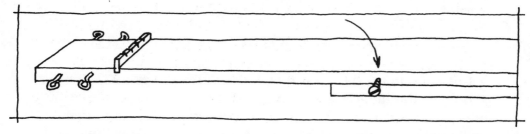

Hammer the five small nails into the end of the post to hold the strings.

Push the post through the banjo head.

If you didn't buy a bridge and are making one out of a small piece of wood, file five grooves about 3/8" apart for the strings. You should carve the bridge to a **thin** triangle shape so it transfers vibrations well.

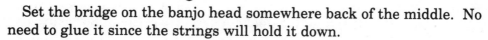

Set the bridge on the banjo head somewhere back of the middle. No need to glue it since the strings will hold it down.

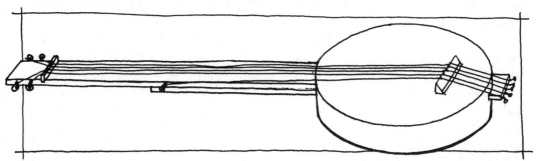

Tie the strings to the nails and screw eyes. I sometimes actually drill tiny holes through the screw eyes to thread the strings. Tune the strings by turning the screw eyes. Position the bridge after all the strings are partially tightened.

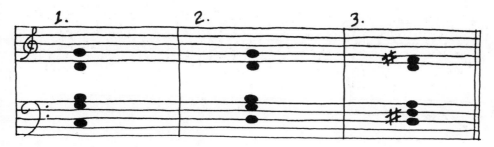

PLAYING TIPS:

The neat thing about the bleach bottle banjo is that it actually plays. The design incorporates the basic necessities of vibration, amplification, and pitch. Hold it like a regular banjo or guitar. Tune it to a pleasing chord. If you are a righty, the right hand strums and the left hand fingers the notes. However, like a "real" banjo, you have to have some prior knowledge in order to make chords and accompany songs. If you have no experience at all you may want to rest the banjo on your lap and play it like a dulcimer. *The Dulcimer Book* by Jean Ritchie (Oak Publications, 33 West 60th St., New York, N.Y. 10023) gives good instructions, but the best way to learn any instrument is from someone else who plays.

THE PEANUT BUTTER PAIL BANJO

After playing the bleach bottle banjo for a while, I wanted a bigger and louder one, so I made one out of a plastic pail, the kind you get in a health-food store that holds 30 lbs of peanut butter. It is made like the bleach bottle banjo but with some significant modifications: The neck is longer than the bleach bottle version because the plastic pail is larger. And you should use light gauge metal banjo strings which are louder than nylon and the notes ring longer. But metal strings create a lot of tension and are likely to pull the tuners out of soft wood, so this banjo neck is made of oak, maple, or even a broken hockey stick (ash). The tuners I use are machine screw eyes (not wood screw eyes), which require that I pre-drill holes for them into the peg head just the right diametre so they will not fall out yet will offer the precision tuning that metal strings require.

I've had a lot of fun with my peanut butter pail banjo. You might have seen me with it on one of the Elephant Shows, playing an old traditional tune called *Cluck Old Hen*. I also play it in the song *Momma Don't 'Low* on the album *Fiddle Up a Tune* !

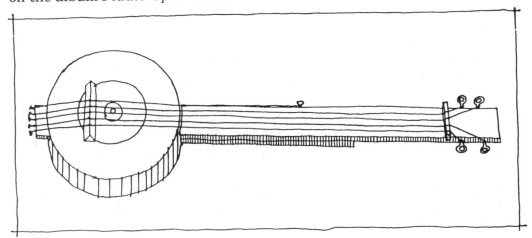

THE PSALTERY

The psaltery has a pure and fragile sound that seems very ancient. Each string you pluck rings and rings, colouring all the notes that come after. The first time I heard Bob Beers play the psaltery I fell in love with its delicate sound. Then again I'm always falling in love with instruments aren't I? They seem to follow me home like stray puppies.

But the psaltery was exceptional. It had an enchanting quality and when Bob played it while his wife and daughter sang, the music would capture me in a magical spell.

Bob's instrument had been built by a Mr. MacKenzie who lived in Minneapolis, Minnesota during the turn of the century. He and his niece, Esther Whitcup, travelled through the United States selling psalteries and giving music lessons. One of those instruments passed through many hands before Bob acquired it in Roundup, Montana in 1954.

There were others like me who had met and heard Bob Beers and who wanted to learn to play the psaltery, but none were to be had. So about twenty years ago a cabinet- and instrument-maker named Michael Autorino began building them for those of us who were bitten by the psaltery bug. I guess Michael made and sold about twenty of them before he died. I have one of his.

Sometimes when I play the psaltery I envision Bob's capable hands plucking the strings instead of my own. I hear his family singing *Dunbarton's Drums*, and I feel the warm sun streaming through the bay window of their country living-room on that spring day in 1966 when I first heard the psaltery's haunting sound.

The psaltery is a box with strings stretched across it. That makes it a relative of the zither, the autoharp, the harpsichord, and the piano. The larger psalteries, such as the one I play on *Friendship Pin* on the *Come On In* album, look very much like hammered dulcimers. The main difference is that you pluck the strings of a psaltery and you strike a hammered dulcimer with little mallets.

To make a successful psaltery it is important to pay attention to the relationship between the string and the box. A cardboard shoe box, for example, is delicate and requires a thin string like a rubber band. A stronger box like a metal cookie container requires a stronger string, like a metal banjo string. Remember that some materials vibrate better than others. A wooden cigar box (if you can find one) vibrates better than a cardboard one.

The string must make contact with the box in such a way as to vibrate the soundboard, i.e., a bridge.

The strings should be tuneable. For example they could be attached to something that turns.

Sometimes it's a good idea to reinforce the box where the tuners are attached, so as to withstand the tension of the strings.

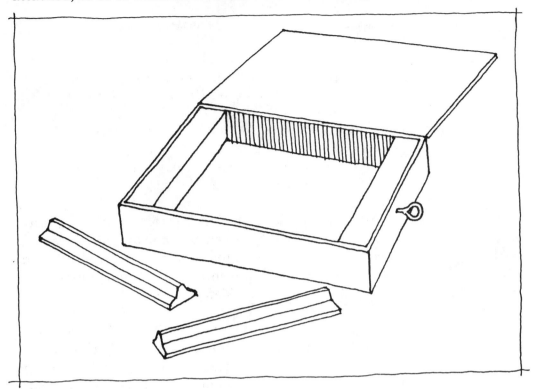

The diagram shows a simple psaltery made from nylon guitar strings or fishing line. The box is a wooden cigar box (use cardboard if you have to), and the pegs are screw eyes

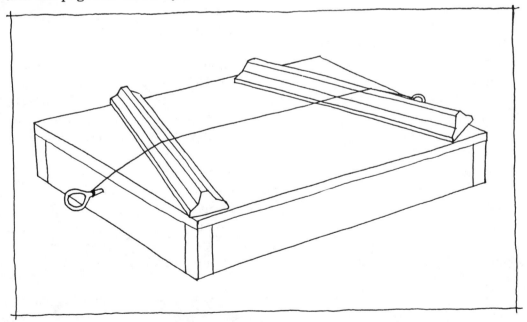

Tune your psaltery in *do*, *re*, *me* fashion, and find pleasing note combinations to accompany your song.

WASHINGTON SQUARE

Fiddles and banjoes aren't only found in the country. In fact, as a teenager I learned to play banjo in downtown New York City; Greenwich Village in fact. Back then on any warm Sunday afternoon you could find a few hundred people gathered around the fountain in Washington Square. There would be a dozen or more clusters of spectators, and at the centre of each group would be a band of two to five musicians. With each band playing a different tune, it created quite a din when heard from a distance. But up-close to each group some neat music could be experienced.

I had been playing banjo night and day for a month when my brother told me about Washington Square, and some of the more common songs that were played there, like *Hard Ain't It Hard*, *Jesse James*, *Hand Me Down My Walking Cane*, and *Ridin On That New River Train*. For two weeks I practised until I could play them pretty good, and on the next Sunday, packed my banjo, scrounged up a dollar for lunch and car fare, and took the subway to Greenwich Village.

The first group I encountered included a mandolinist, three guitarists, and a lead singer who also played a washtub. He and the instrument fascinated me. (I later learned his name was Lionel Kilburg, well known for popularizing the washtub in those days.) I wound my way through a dozen spectators and stood just outside the circle, dying to play but apprehensive about jumping in. When Lionel looked up from the bass and saw the banjo in my hands his eyes lit up.

"Come on in," he said. "Get tuned. What songs do you know?"

"*New River Train?*"

"Okay," his voice was pleasant. "1...and...2...and...*Ridin' on that New River Train...*"

The band was off and running. I reached up to tune my banjo but my fingers missed the peg. I reached again... missed again. I glanced up expecting to see that the peg head had dropped off or something. But there it was, like always, right at the end of the banjo neck. My hand, however, was shaking like a leaf. "Gosh," I thought, "I must be nervous." My heart was beating like a hammer. The crowd was staring at me.

"Banjo tuned yet?" It was Lionel. They had come to the instrumental break.

"Just a sec."

The mandolin player took the break. I forced my fingers to grab the peg and hold on. I turned it... too high, then too low. Finally got it. Four more strings to go.

"Banjo ready?"

Holy Smokes. They were practically to the end of the song. I tried to keep tuning but my hands wouldn't stop shaking. The fifth string wouldn't hold its tune and kept going flat like a tire with a hole in it. Lionel finished *New River Train* and blended it into *Jesse James*. The crowd seemed to have swelled to a multitude. A thousand eyes, smirking, leering, drilling into me.

"Banjo ready?"

Darn! It was Lionel again. Now they were playing *Hand Me Down My Walking Cane*. Lionel sang every verse he knew and repeated it twice. The guitars and the mandolin had each taken their breaks. Even Lionel had played one on the bass.

There! Finally in tune. The band had started into *Hard Ain't it Hard*, my favourite song; the only one I could play Scruggs Style. I loved Scruggs picking because it was fast, loud, and impressive. Your fingers go a mile-a-minute and the melody jumps out like fireworks. I waited for my break.

"Banjo ready?"

I nodded to Lionel. The chorus came to an end and he looked at me. The band looked at me. The crowd looked at me. The entire world, the angels in the heavens, all the greek gods, even Zeus himself all stared down with their mighty stares, awaiting my debut. Flo Ziegfield was there. So was the music critic for the *New York Times*. Beethoven, President Eisenhower, and Mrs. Zeckster, my sixth grade teacher who had expected great things of me... all staring at me.

My hands froze. Solid as a rock. For the last ten minutes I hadn't been able to hold them still while I'd been trying to tune. Now they wouldn't budge. Not a chord. Not a note. Not a peep. Not even a mini-peep.

You should have seen me slinking back to the subway. My sweat-soaked shirt sticking to my back. You could have poured me through the cracks in the side-walk I was so humiliated.

When I got home my mom asked me how it went.

"Great," I said.

The next Sunday when I returned to The Square, Lionel welcomed me back with a big smile and this time I was able to play a few tunes with the band. In no time I was making new friends, learning new songs, and making my way through adolescence living for the Sundays of Washington Square.

THE BROWNIE BASS

To this day Lionel Killberg is the best washtub bass player I've ever heard. He called his instrument a "Brownie Bass." It was modified with a spring to keep the pole upright. Lionel played it in true professional fashion and could make it sound like a real bass fiddle. He didn't raise and lower the pitch by tightening and loosening the string, but instead he changed the string length by running his hand up and down the pole. This helped keep the quality of tone equal for each note. It's a harder way of playing but the results are more like a real bass fiddle.

I used to laugh at old timers who would talk about "the good old days." Not any more. Good quality materials for a washtub bass are becoming expensive and hard to find. The best sounding string is a braided cotton clothesline or sash cord about 1/4" in diameter. Polypropylene or nylon rope is not as loud. You can still buy washtubs in hardware stores but the "heavy duty" washtub available today is considerably thinner than even a few years ago. The thin ones don't sound as good and they wear out fast. You might be able to find a good older washtub in grandma's basement or a second-hand store.

I'm told that "Wheeling Steels" or "Reeves" are good makes. A #2 size tub gives a good range of notes, and a #3 will play much lower notes. Someone brought a washtub bass that was made out of plywood to one of my concerts. It sounded great.

THE WASHTUB BASS

YOU NEED:

— A washtub or similar container. If you're unable to find a washtub, use a waste basket or pail but note that metal is best, and the bigger diameter the better.
— 1 metal washer (approx 1")
— 1 broom handle (length depending on size of player)
— Strong cord of about the same length. One-quarter inch braided cotton clothesline or sash cord works best.
— 1 thin 3" nail
— 1 fat nail
— A hammer
— A saw
— A drill
— Rat tail and triangle files

HERE'S WHAT TO DO:

Use the saw and triangle file to cut a groove along the flat end of the broom handle which will fit the lip of the tub.

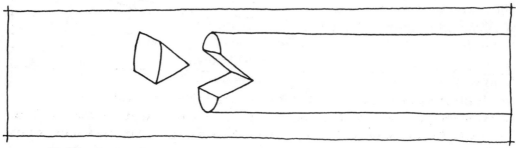

Drill a hole in broomstick end as shown. (Or attach a nail or screw to the end.)

Tie the washer to one end of the cord. Draw the string through the hole in the tub so that the washer end is left on the inside. The washer stops the cord from being pulled through the hole.

With the hammer and fat nail make a hole in the centre of the tub wide enough for the cord to fit through. Use the rat tail file to file the edge of the hole smooth so that it won't cut the cord.

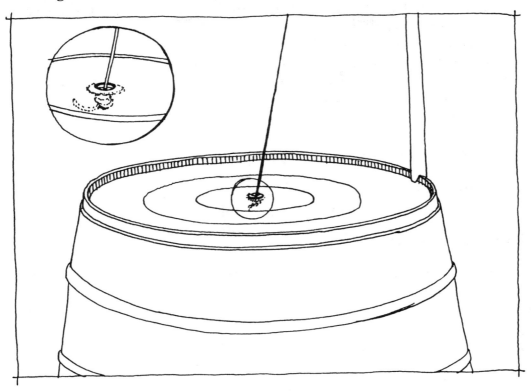

Fit the grooved end of the handle to the rim of the tub.

String the other end of the cord through the hole at the top (or tie to nail). Experiment with the length. The cord should be tied short since it's going to stretch.

HOW TO PLAY YOUR WASHTUB BASS:

If you're a righty, hold the pole in your left hand and pluck the string with your right. Put your right foot on the lip of the tub to hold it still. Try to keep your foot off the vibrating surface.

HOW TO CHANGE THE NOTES:

The simplest way to change notes is by pulling on the pole. As the tension increases, the note goes higher. For the more advanced player, notes can be changed by changing the length of the string: grip the string to the pole with your left hand and slide it up and down the pole. Keep the pole at a constant angle to the tub. When you use this technique the quality of the notes is more consistant.

If your hands get sore while learning this instrument, you can wear gloves or tape up your fingers.

RELATED INSTRUMENTS

Here's a home-made instrument you don't see around much: the African pit-harp or earth bow (also called the mosquito drum in Haiti). People surmise that it is the ancestor to the washtub bass. All you need is a sapling growing in a field and a large animal skin.

The earth bow consists of a shallow hole dug next to a sapling tree, an animal skin stretched over the hole and pegged down, and then a long animal sinew connecting the top of the sapling to the skin held fast by a small twig.

The earth makes a very good resonator of sound, giving a deep mellow colour to the tone. This instrument can be re-constructed using a 7' flexible pole dug into the ground, 4'-5' of string or wire, a pit covering made of rubber, leather skins, a sheet of metal, or thin sheet of plywood, stakes or tent pegs. If you make one, send me a picture and tape of it.

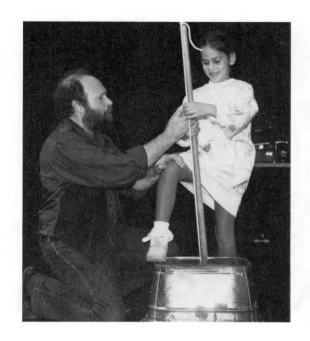

FIDDLES AND RATTLESNAKES

There's a rattlesnake rattle inside my fiddle. I put it there. It's very good luck. Old timers used to put a rattle in their fiddles to keep out the devil. You see, people used to think that the fiddle was the devil's instrument because when it played it would make you dance, even if you didn't want to. And some people thought that dancing was sinful. If you ask me I'd say that the rattle inside my fiddle works, because ever since I put it there I haven't seen any fiery-red creatures with horns and long tails.

When I was younger I learned a lot about fiddles, rattles, and tunes from Bob Beers. He taught me many tunes that he had learned from his grandfather, George Sullivan. Saturday night musical parties were a weekly event at the Sullivan homestead. George was a wonderful fiddler. It was George Sullivan who taught Bob about rattlesnake rattles. So that tradition stretches back four generations for me. I play some tunes exactly the way George Sullivan did, even though I never met him. In fact, both Bob and George died quite a while ago.

When I play their music, I'm reminded that my fiddle contains a bit of their spirit. And I wonder if the rattlesnake rattle might be the place where the spirits of the old timers dwell.

My fiddle seems to have a mind of its own. Sometimes I can't tell if I'm playing it, or if it's playing me. There are times when I'm really excited to fiddle up a tune but when I open the case the fiddle looks hard and cold, like ice. And no matter how I try I can't keep it from sounding squeaky and squalky. Then I can remember a time when it was five o'clock in the morning and I was sound asleep. Suddenly something woke me up and I found myself staring at the fiddle case. Half asleep I opened it and the first rays of dawn softly caressed the tanned wood, making the fiddle look warm and fuzzy. I picked it up and drew the bow across the strings. Beautiful soft music filled the room.

It's strange. Maybe it was George Sullivan's spirit rustling around in that rattlesnake rattle, feeling restless and wanting to play.

As a young boy, Bob Beers spent many vacations at the Sullivan farm in North Freedom, Wisconsin. He came to love the country, the music, and the old ways. Of the many stories that Bob told me, let me pass one on.

THE GREAT HIGH WIND

Bob was studying violin at university when a message summoned him to the farm. The long train ride through the night gave him lots of time to wonder about Grandma's message, and why she sent for him in mid-term. He arrived in North Freedom early the next day. Entering through the kitchen, Bob embraced Grandma's frail body, and noticed that the parlour door was open, the potbelly stove ablaze. Grandpa Sullivan, now ninety-one, sat alone on the piano bench, fiddle in hand, the way Bob had seen him at countless Saturday night parties. But on this morning he sat alone. Bob plopped down in front of his grandfather, who began to play.

George Sullivan spoke not a word, but fiddled tune after tune, each melody different from the one before. Bob recognized most from the Saturday night gatherings but there were some he had never heard before. As morning grew into afternoon the notes continued to tumble out of Grandpa's fiddle as if in some desperate way the old man was trying to recapture the musical memories of an entire lifetime.

Even as day retreated into evening the fiddle music still kept coming. It was not until darkness had fallen that Grandpa Sullivan played one final tune: *The Great High Wind*. Bob had heard his grandfather play *The Great High Wind* many times as a rousing song. But on this night George Sullivan did not sing, and he played it slowly... almost mournfully... like a dirge.

When he finished, he stood and placed his fiddle in Bob's hands. Without a word, he turned and left the room.

Grandpa Sullivan never played the fiddle again.

Now don't get me wrong. The old man didn't die on that day. He lived to the ripe old age of ninety-seven, and the townsfolk of North Freedom built him a bench in the town square to sit and enjoy... their way of saying thankyou for a lifetime of the best fiddling a hundred miles around.

Bob Beers taught me *The Great High Wind*. In fact you can hear it on one of my albums. I play it fast and lively, more like the way it was so often played on Saturday nights. But Bob also taught me the way his grandfather played it on the day he received Grandpa's fiddle. Sometimes when I play it in that slow and mournful way I can feel old George Sullivan sitting in the room with me, his spirit overflowing the fiddle, freed for an instant from its home in the rattlesnake rattle.

As for Grandpa's old fiddle, it's still going strong. Bob Beers made good use of it until he died and now his niece, George's great-granddaughter, has it. I understand she plays in the St. Louis Symphony and is not too bad either, by all accounts.

Just one last note.... Many years ago on a cold, windswept morning in early spring I found myself in the tiny village of North Freedom, and I visited George Sullivan's grave. It sits among a few dozen others beside an ancient, wooden one-room church. Among the gravestones I recognized the names of some of the neighbours who shared those musical soirees of years gone by. I can't really describe to you the strange wave of emotion that rocked me as I stood above the bones of the man that played *The Great High Wind*.

THE CORNSTALK FIDDLE

Bob Beers was an incredible showman and he could keep kids fascinated for hours with his tall tales and nonsense songs. Bob showed me all sorts of useful things, like how to trap a rabbit with a box and a few sticks, how to hypnotize a frog by looking deep into its eyes, and how to lullaby a chicken to sleep.

Bob and his daughter, Martha, played all sorts of instruments and some were very unusual. One of these was the cornstalk fiddle. They made a big show of rosining the bow, "tuning" the fiddle, and getting all ready to play. But when Martha played all the fiddle did was make a squeaking, scraping noise that hurt your teeth.

I have tried without success to make notes with the cornstalk fiddle and I've never seen anyone do it. If there are any old timers out there who can correct me, please do, but I say the cornstalk fiddle is simply a screeky, scrawky rhythm instrument, all-be-it fun to play and fascinating to watch. You can hear me play the cornstalk fiddle on the album, *Fiddle Up a Tune* and I also show how to make one on my video, *Makin Music With Eric*.

YOU NEED:

— A 1' (approx.) section of cornstalk, the fatter the better. Look for one at the end of summer or try growing one in your backyard.
— 2 small pieces of stalk for bridges
— A springy branch, aproximately 1 1/2' -2' long
— A shoestring (rough cotton, not nylon)
— Violin rosin
— A utility knife

HERE'S WHAT TO DO:

Cut a double section from the cornstalk leaving a node at each end. (A node is the bumpy place that the leaves grow out of.)

Look for the groove running along the sections. In one section, cut away from under the ridges on either side of this groove so that two "strings" of cornstalk remain. Make sure you leave the strings attached at both ends, and keep the strings wide enough so they don't break.

Cut two small bridges from an unused part of the stalk and insert them gently under the strings at each end to raise them off the cornstalk.

Tie the shoestring to the ends of the springy branch and bend to make a bow. You may want to notch each end of the bow to keep the shoestring in place.

Rosin the shoestring a lot with regular violin rosin.

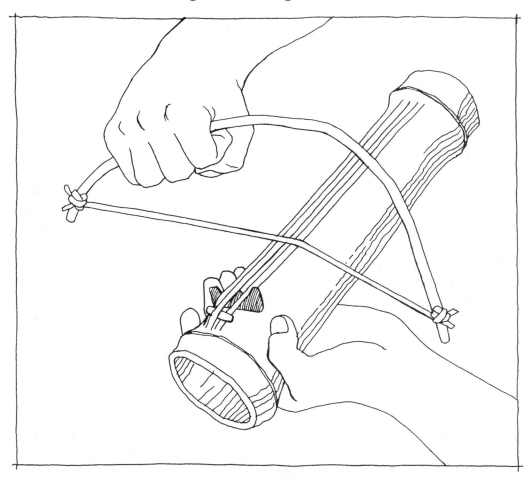

HOW TO PLAY YOUR CORNSTALK FIDDLE:

Just draw the bow string across fiddle strings to the rhythm of the music. Sometimes it helps to have cotton in your ears.

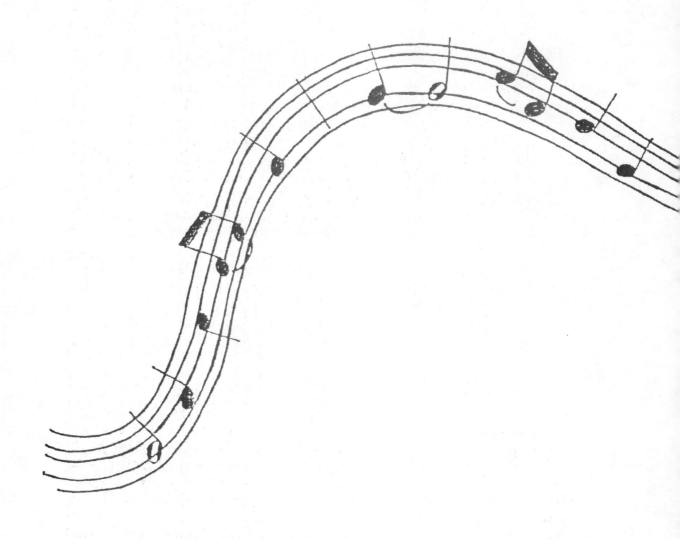

HORNS

The "horn" family of instruments got it's name from the animal horns that these instruments were originally made of. Later they became known as "brass" because they were often made of that metal. My home-made horn is called a "Sewerphone." Guess what it's made of.

To play a horn, don't just blow into it, the air won't vibrate. You have to buzz your lips by closing them and blowing without using your vocal chords. A good thought is to try to imagine spitting a little speck of dust off of your upper lip. **The mouthpiece** of the horn helps pucker your lips to give a better sound and make it easier to change pitch. One way to change pitch while playing a horn is to loosen and tighten your lips. The more **tubing** you add to your horn, the lower the over-all pitch becomes. By adding a **bell** you can amplify the sound.

So remember, to make a horn-type instrument you need three basic parts: A mouthpiece, tubing, and a bell.

Before going into my infamous sewerphone I'll first describe an easier horn to make.

THE HOSE HORN

Don't throw out that old leaky garden hose. Salvage part of it for a hose horn.

YOU NEED:

— A hose nozzle
— A length of old garden hose
— A plastic or metal funnel
— Duct tape (or similar heavy tape)
— A utility knife

HERE'S WHAT TO DO:

A simple, straight hose nozzle as pictured makes a good mouthpiece. Buzz your lips into the wide end. If no sound comes out but instead your cheeks turn red and your eyes get bulgey, perhaps the nozzle is screwed shut instead of open.

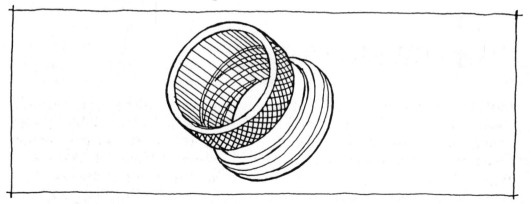

Cut the brass fitting off one end of the garden hose so you can push the small end of the nozzle into it.

Cut the hose to the desired length using a utility knife. An adult should supervise or help with this. Before deciding what length of hose to cut, remember that the longer the hose is, the lower the range of notes. Experiment by first trying a very long piece and gradually cutting it shorter to the length you like. Or make a few different lengths for various keys. I prefer about 10' which seems to give the instrument a nice pitch range without being difficult to play. If the hose is unmanageably long, coil it up and tape it. Coiling a tube won't change the pitch. If a tuba was stretched out straight it would be about 18' long. Coiling your instrument is cheaper than renting a stretch limo every time you want to take it somewhere.

Push the funnel into the other end.

Wrap the joints with duct tape. They should be as airtight as possible. Bingo, your hose horn is ready.

Now for a harder one.

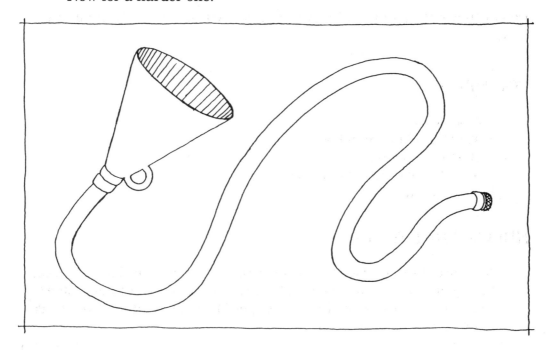

THE SEWERPHONE

Half the fun of a home-made instrument is its looks. Although the sewerphone is essentially no different from the hose horn, its formidable appearance makes the playing of it seem more amazing. You can see me and my friend, the Reverend Ken play dueling tubas on my TV special, *The Eric Nagler Generic Family Music Holiday Special*. The sound of the two instruments, in my humble opinion, is simply terrible. But they look rather spectacular, and the effect is quite entertaining.

People think I invented the sewerphone, but actually I got the idea for my instrument from the Reverend Ken. His sewerphone uses a kitchen sink for a bell. The cheapest used kitchen sink I could find was twenty bucks (too expensive for any home-made instrument), so I opted for a three-dollar washing machine agitator instead. I think it looks classier anyway.

A friendly salesperson in a plumbing supply store helped me with my first sewerphone. I had no idea there were so many different sorts of fittings, joints, and shapes made of ABS (a type of plastic) drainpipe. Most of the larger hardware stores carry everything you need.

I use a regular trombone mouthpiece. A hose nozzle works O.K., but the mouthpiece works better.

Here's how to make one.

YOU NEED:

—A hose nozzle (or trombone mouthpiece)
—About 10' of ABS drainpipe. It doesn't matter how wide the tube is.
My present one is 1 1/2".
—Curved fittings, plugs, adapters, etc. according to your design.
—A resonator, such as a washing machine agitator or funnel. Or be like
the Reverend Ken and use a kitchen sink.
[INSERT]
—ABS cleaner and cement. Use these poisonous materials with adult
supervision.
—A small paint brush for the cement and a rag for the cleaner.

HERE'S WHAT TO DO:

Cut the straight ABS pipe into about four equal lengths. Lay out the
pieces and fit them together without glue at first, until you are sure
you have found a pattern that is comfortable to play and hold. Then
take the pieces apart one at a time and re-assemble using the ABS
cleaner and cement. It's best if all joints are airtight.

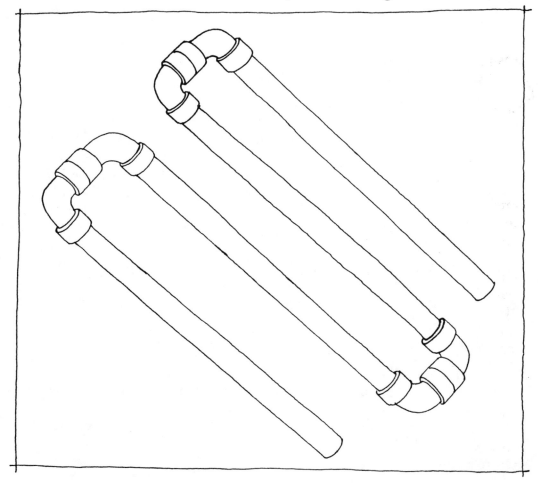

You can get an adapter that attaches ABS pipe to copper tube, into which you can fit your mouthpiece. Tape wrapped around the shaft of the mouthpiece can help to make an airtight fit. I don't glue in the mouthpiece because I want to be able to remove it during travel.

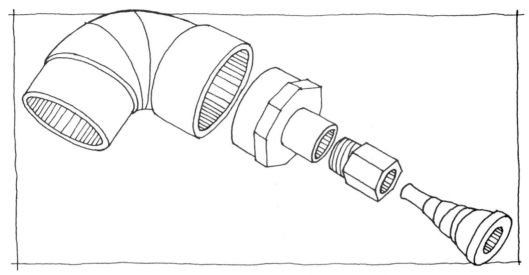

Fit the bell-shaped resonator onto the other end of the pipe. The agitator I found was a perfect size to take an ABS adapter with a screw thread. Therefore I can remove my agitator to facilitate travel. Unfortunately the darn thing won't fit into any of my luggage, so I'm forever carrying it past skeptical airport security guards, amused stewardesses, and amazed passengers.

THE JUG

One can't really write a home-made instrument book without describing the jug. After all, the term "jug band" refers to a type of music that thrives on home-made instruments. It's simply a jug made of glass, ceramic, or stoneware. Even a plastic milk jug will do just fine.

HOW TO PLAY YOUR JUG:

Play it by buzzing your lips (as you would a horn-type instrument) into the mouth of the jug. Angle the jug until you get a resonant sound. Change the pitch by tightening and loosening your lips as you would if you were playing a horn-type instrument.

A friend of mine came up with an invention called the slide water jug, a modification of the usual jug. It is supposed to be easier to change pitch, but my friend has never actually made a slide water jug and neither have I. I can just see water spilling all over the kitchen floor and me in big trouble.... Instead, why don't you try it and let me know what happens.

THE SLIDE WATER JUG

YOU NEED:

— A plastic jug or bleach bottle
— A utility knife
— A bucket, larger than the jug
— Water

HERE'S WHAT TO DO:

Cut out the bottom of the plastic jug with a utility knife. Put water in
the bucket until it is about 3/4 full.

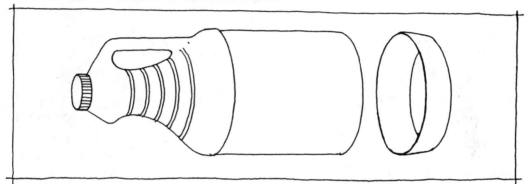

HOW TO PLAY YOUR SLIDE WATER JUG:

Push the jug down into the water and buzz as you would any ordinary
jug. Move the jug up and down at different levels in the water while
buzzing to change the pitch.

POP BOTTLE WHISTLES

You may know that if you blow across the mouth of a pop bottle you can get a note. Position the lip of the bottle just under your lower lip, pucker slightly, and blow a jet of air across and into the bottle. The pitch of the note has to do with the ratio of pop in your tummy and pop left in the bottle.

This one definitely works: My friend Joe Hampson can play tunes with a pop bottle that has had about one large gulp removed. He uses a pop bottle that's exactly the same size as a beer bottle. By changing the shape of his lips and tilting the bottle, he can play an entire scale of notes.

OLD CHARLIE

As a kid I would spend July and August at the cottage. There were mountains, lakes, forests, and fields... lots of opportunity for adventure.

Once or twice each summer I would see a strange-looking man walking in long, silent strides along our country lane. He was very tall and thin with brown, wrinkled skin, and an enormous hooked nose that blocked the sun from the corncob pipe that hung from his lips. His clothes were old and dark, stained with grass and grease. He wore a tattered derby hat and a lumberman's plaid shirt. His vest was of raw brown leather, and over his shoulder hung a weathered pouch. He always carried a long rod, like a shepherd's staff.

I kept my distance. Sometimes he'd nod to me as he passed. His face seemed kind enough, but I was a bit afraid of him because he looked so different. My parents didn't know who he was, but my friend Jeffrey said he was called Old Charlie.

"They say he's half Indian, and he lives somewhere in the woods beyond Scoffield's farm."

No one else seemed to know much about him, and, other than our brief encounters on the road, I never saw Old Charlie around anywhere... except once.

That summer I was 11, and one hot and humid day I decided to do some lazy fishing. I picked a few worms from under rocks, put a line and a few hooks in a bag, tied it to my handle bars, and headed for the dump road. A few kilometres from our house there was a creek with a deep pool. If you leaned over the ledge of the rock overlooking the pool you could see nice fat trout wagging their tails lazily against the current.

It was mid-afternoon. I didn't see any fish, but threw my line in anyway, wound it around my finger, and lay on the rock watching the swirls of water. With the sun toasting my back, I dreamed of trout frying in the pan, and my mouth started watering in anticipation.

"They ain't gonna be there this time o' day," came a voice from across the pool. My head jerked up, and to my surprise there was Old Charlie, his corncob pipe hanging from his mouth, sitting in the shade of a willow tree, whittling on his staff.

"And anyway, these trout've been fished at so much any of em's stupid enough to go for your scrawny little worms've been caught and et long before you pulled on your first pair of long pants."

I was still a little stunned by the way Charlie had seemed to materialize from thin air and his words sort of drifted by me.

"Ya see," he continued, "a trout's not gonna like the warm sunny water this time a day. They's either gone deeper or upstream... maybe they's even over on this side in the shade of the overhangs."

I felt like a real fool. Anyone who fishes knows that only sunfish are attracted to such heat.

"You can try over here if you've a mind." Charlie had a kind voice and it would have been terribly impolite to turn down his invitation, so I crossed the small bridge and sat down under the willow beside Old Charlie. He interupted his whittling to cut a branch for me to tie my line to.

We talked about fish and worms, and lots of stuff. I told him about people I'd seen hunting worms at night, with flashlights taped to their hats and coffee cans strapped to their ankles. They would roam the city lawns at night, bent over double, picking worms and dropping them in the cans. Charlie laughed at such a silly sight and described a much easier way to catch worms using powdered mustard and water. You pour the mixture down their holes and they come shooting out like geysers. He showed me how to spot a worm hole by the little turds that surround them. They looked like tiny volcanoes.

Old Charlie went back to carving on his staff without saying any more about worms. He passed it to me for a closer look. It was beautiful! On it he'd carved all sorts of things. There was a milk snake and a partridge, a chevron of geese, a fox, ants, flowers, and just dozens of exquisitely sculpted miniatures of what you might see in the woods and fields. At the top he'd carved a magnificent oak tree with branches that reached majestically around the thickest part of the pole.

Charlie let me slice a little chip out of the rod, and then he transformed it into the wing of an eagle, soaring high over a field. In the field he began to work on a mouse, hiding behind a rock.

Charlie's knife was very sharp. He showed me how he honed it on a stone he kept in his pocket, using spit as a lubricant. "Some spit cuts better 'n others," he said. "Depends on what you eat. Milk with your coffee don't do no good for spit." Well, I drank a fair amount of milk in those days and no coffee at all, but my spit cut pretty good and gave a sharp edge to the blade. Charlie and I put it down to the fact that I also drank a lot of pop.

Then Old Charlie reached in his pouch, pulled out a small, smokey flavoured roast chicken to share. At least I think it was a chicken. After we ate, Old Charlie reached up and cut a piece of willow branch about as thick as my thumb and a few inches long, shaved some bark off one end and notched the other. Then he soaked the stick in the stream for a few minutes. When he took it out, he rubbed the stick over and over with the handle of his knife. Then with one sharp thump on a rock the loose bark slid off in one tubular piece, and Charlie proceeded to make a little slide whistle. He put down his corncob pipe and played me a tune as I munched on a leg of bird under the willow tree. The tune was called *The Wee Herd's Whistle*.

When the song was through, he passed the whistle over for me to try. I was just getting the hang of it when my fishing rod suddenly began to shake. A bite! I threw down the whistle and grabbed the pole before it got dragged into the pool. The trout was big and the rod slender. I had to play the fish a bit before getting it close to the edge so that Charlie could smack it out of the water and up onto the bank. It was a beauty, about as long as my arm! Charlie shook his head in disbelief as we admired the fine catch.

"That fish must have taken your poor old water-logged worm out of sheer disbelief that anyone in his right mind would be fishing with anything that sick lookin'! I can't figure it any other way."

I'd gotten so caught up in fishing, whittling, and whistles that, before I realized, the afternoon had disappeared and dusk was fast approaching. It was time to get home, and quick! I looked at the fish and at Charlie. Then I handed it to him as a payment for all the things I'd learned that day.

"No thanks, take it home to your parents. Maybe it'll make up for you bein' late. And this is for you," he said handing me the whistle he'd made.

I didn't see Old Charlie again that summer. The next summer we passed him on the highway once while driving into town. I could only wave. I told my dad that was Old Charlie, the wonderful wood carver that lived in the.... Gee, I'd never thought to ask Old Charlie if it was true that he lived in a shack behind Homer's farm. I guess I'd sort of known Charlie would not want to talk about his personal life.

The following year we rented out the cottage and took a trip across the country so it wasn't until part-way through the next summer that I realized I hadn't seen Old Charlie around anywhere. I asked my friend Jeffrey about him.

"Old Charlie? Why he passed away two winters ago." My heart took a quick beat. I'd been afraid he was going to say that.

"Did you ever find out where he lived?" I asked.

"No, never did, but I always saw him coming or going from the same direction on the Old Scoffield Road."

So Old Charlie went out of my life, but I'd think of him and me under that willow tree whenever I'd sharpen a knife or carve a branch, or when I'd hunt worms with the old mustard water trick. And of course, I'd always think of him whenever I made a willow whistle.

Years later, as a young man, I was visiting my parents at the cottage and decided to take a long hike through my old haunts on Homer's farm. There were the three giant rocks that we used to climb, and the old stone fence where I'd caught a huge black snake one sunny afternoon, the ball field, the picnic spots ... lots of things to trigger fond memories. I guess my longer legs brought me further than I used to walk as a kid because presently I found myself in unfamiliar territory. I headed uphill to get my bearings and came to a clearing I'd never known about before. In the middle was a giant oak tree. Something about it gave me the chills. Then it struck me. I was looking at the very tree that I had seen carved into Old Charlie's staff. I was in his territory.

It didn't take me long to find the shack, which sat amid a stand of maples not far from the clearing. Time had done it's work: the windows were broken and the roof had caved in on one side. I walked through the open doorway. The floor was dirt, and there was no stove beneath the pipes that still hung from a rusty bent coat hanger attached to one of the few remaining rafters. A broken chair that had been fashioned from bent honeysuckle wood, a few rusty pots, and an old empty cupboard were about all that was left of the furniture. I over-turned a few boards hoping to find Old Charlie's rod, his pouch, or even a piece of clothing I might recognize to prove this really was his shack, but there was nothing. That is until I turned to leave. There, under the old honeysuckle chair, half-buried in the earth, was Old Charlie's corncob pipe.

THE WILLOW SLIDE WHISTLE

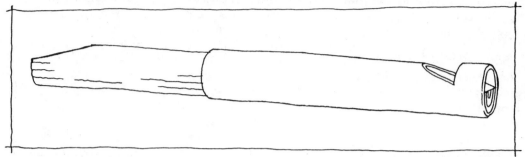

The neat thing about this instrument is that all you need is a willow tree and a knife. Of course in some places willow trees are scarcer than hardware stores. So I often make slide whistles from copper or plastic tubing and a piece of dowel, even a fat plastic straw and a pencil. The principle of the mouthpiece is the same for most whistles. You'll find a description of the hardware store slide whistle further on. I like the hardware store version because it is actually easier to make and has a greater range of notes than the traditional instrument.

   I often make a slide whistle when I'm bored or watching TV... or fishing, because it takes some mindless patience. They are best made in the spring when the sap is running. In other seasons, soak the branch in water for a day so the bark will slip off with less difficulty. Willow is best because the bark is thick. American ash is good too. The bark is the tube of the whistle, and the inside (the wood) is the plunger.

YOU NEED:

   — A straight piece of willow branch without knots, no more than 5" long and about 1/2" in diameter.
   — A utility knife

HERE'S WHAT TO DO:

   Measure about 1/2" from an end and cut around the branch through the bark but not through the wood. Remove the bark from this end and discard it.
   Measure about 1/2" from the other end and cut a notch about 1/4" deep.

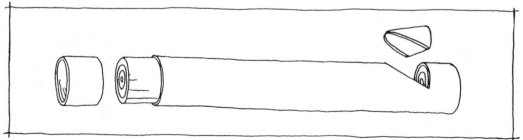

Firmly rub the bark all over with the rounded handle of a knife. Squeeze, roll, and twist it until the bark starts to come loose from the wood. This is the hardest part. You need a lot of patience because you must be sure not to split the bark in the process. When the bark seems pretty loose, thump the barkless end on a hard surface until it slides off.

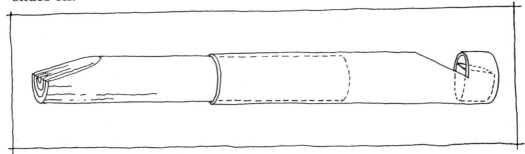

Slice off a little strip of wood between the notch and the end to allow an air passage. Then chop off the rest and plug it into the blowing end of the tube. Slide the wood back into the bark.

HOW TO PLAY YOUR SLIDE WHISTLE:

Play it like any slide whistle, blowing into the space above the plug and sliding the plunger in and out. When the plunger is in, the tube is short and so the pitch of the instrument is high. When the plunger is out, the pitch is low.

THE HARDWARE STORE VERSION

YOU NEED:

— A section of 1/2" copper tubing about 10" long. (If the hardware store has more than one quality, get the thinnest)
— A section of 1/2" wooden dowelling 1" long, or a cork that you can shape to fit snugly into the tube. I sometimes wrap tape around the wooden dowel to make it fit.
— A piece of 1/4" wooden dowelling 1 1/2' long, or any similar straight stick.
— A cellulose sponge. I find most plastic and synthetic sponges are too porous. You need a dense sponge
— Glue such as five-minute epoxy or an instant bonding glue like Crazy Glue for wood and leather.
— A triangle metal file
— A round metal file
— A sharp knife
— A nail or awl

HERE'S WHAT TO DO:

Using the file, make a triangular slot in the tube about 1" from one end. Angle the file so that the slot looks like the diagram.

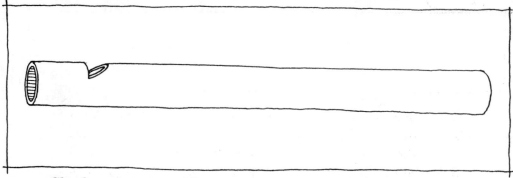

Check your copper tube to make sure that the inside edges are smooth. Sometimes there are crimps in the metal because of the way it's been cut. If this is so, you must file these inside edges smooth with a round metal file so the plug will fit snugly.

Shape the dowel or cork into a plug that will fit into the tube snugly.

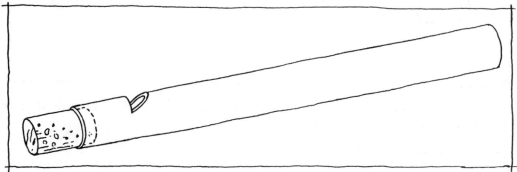

Cut a flat surface along the plug on an angle so that when you blow into the tube, some air will be directed out through the slot and some will stay in the tube.

Adjust the plug in the tube so that you get a good sound. Keep your finger over the other end of the tube when you blow. With the plug in the right place you can glue it if you want, but really it should be snug enough without glue. Air leaks are not good.

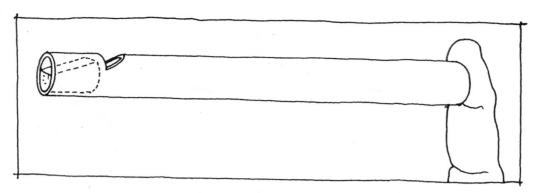

Cut a piece of sponge about 1" long and round it with the knife or scissors until it's slightly wider than the diameter of the tube. The sponge, when wet, must be able to slide easily but not leak air.

With the nail or awl, punch a hole through the sponge and glue it to the long stick.

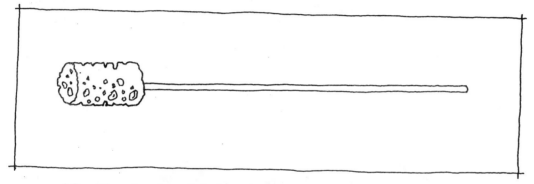

After the glue has dried, wet the sponge thoroughly and slide it into the tube.

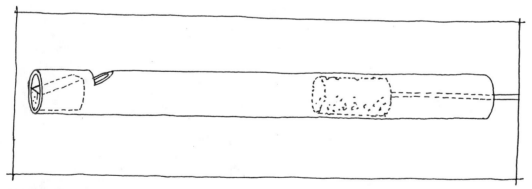

PLAYING TIP:

Make sure the sponge is kept wet so that it will slide easily.

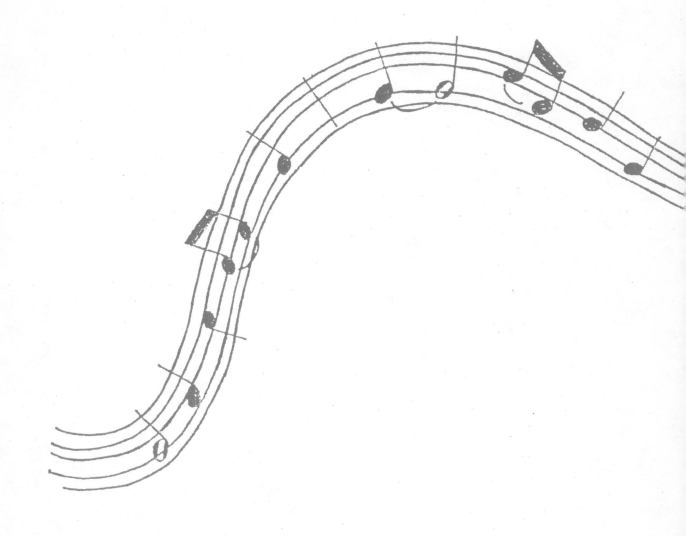

THE VOICE

I don't know why people frequently mistake me for Bram Morrison. So what if we are about the same age and size, both have beards and moustaches, and are both musicians on *The Elephant Show*. Our moms can tell us apart real easy.

One day while *The Elephant Show* was shooting in downtown Toronto and we were on a break, I noticed an old acquaintance of mine talking to Bram... which surprised me because I didn't think he knew Bram.

"My Eric, how you've changed!" I heard him say. "Your hair is much darker, you've lost a little weight, and in fact you've even grown a bit. And your clothes... why I've never seen you look so dapper."

"I'm not Eric, I'm Bram." Bram explained.

"Amazing!" my friend replied, "You've even changed your name!"

People recognize us in different ways and our voice is one of them. A voice is as individual as a fingerprint. Perhaps that's why some people find it scary and vulnerable to sing. Our voice often reveals what's in our hearts.

The voice follows the same rules of vibration and amplification as any other instrument. Voice sounds are formed by air moving through the vocal chords, lips, and teeth. The vocal chords are two flaps of elastic tissue controlled by muscles located in the throat just about where the Adam's apple is. You can feel them vibrating if you place your hand on your throat and hum. When we breathe, the vocal chords are loose and lay out of the way; but when we want to talk or sing, our muscles tighten the vocal chords and they move close together to form a little slit through which the air passes. They work just like an instrument. When the cords are tight and vibrate quickly, the pitch is high; and when they are relaxed, the vibration is slower and the pitch is lower.

Why do kids have higher voices than adults? Because their vocal chords are shorter and vibrate more rapidly than adult's vocal chords. Here's something to try to see how your vocal chords work.

YOU NEED:

— An elastic band
— A broken balloon
— A funnel
— A razor blade

HERE'S WHAT TO DO:

Stretch the balloon over the mouth of the funnel and secure it with the elastic band. With the razor blade make a small slit in the balloon. Blow through the nozzle and watch what happens to the balloon as the air blows through the slit. Try stretching the balloon tighter and blowing again. Also try it after cutting the slit a little bigger.

The balloon vibrates similarly to the way your vocal chords vibrate.

THE COMB KAZOO

When I invite people up on stage to play with me, the comb kazoo is the instrument that takes the most courage because you don't just blow into it; you have to use your voice to play it.

A kazoo is more like an "amplifier" than an instrument. It uses a little piece of wax paper and a tube to change the sound of your voice and make it a little louder.

You can buy a kazoo in a music store, but don't. It's simple to make your own for free. All it takes is a comb and a piece of wax paper about 6" long.

HERE'S WHAT TO DO:

Fold the waxed paper over the comb once. Keep the paper stretched tight. Make an "oooo" sound with your lips and voice. Don't blow! It's your vocal chords that vibrate the air. Bring the kazoo close to your mouth and just touch it to your lips so you can feel it tickle.

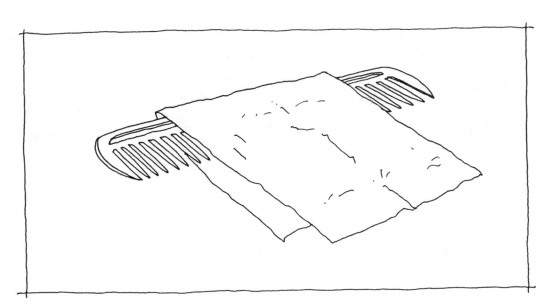

Most people hum into their kazoos, but there are many different things to do to make the sound more interesting. Try imitating a horn, going "wah, wah" or even wailing. You can push all sorts of mouth sounds through the kazoo and make some interesting music.

DOWN BY THE RIVERSIDE

December, 1986

Let me finish this book with a true story that taught me a lot about the power of the voice, both in music and in speech. A long time ago I travelled to a far-away land called Mississippi, where there was a man named the Reverend Martin Luther King Jr. He was registering people to vote, and he had invited anyone who wanted to come to Mississippi to help. It seems that most of the people who lived in Mississippi were black, but they were not being treated very well. Dr. King figured that if the black people could vote they would be treated better. So he started marching down the road to let black people know it was time to ´ vote. And I went to see if I could lend a hand and, well, just for the adventure.

I travelled for several days before I found the little band of marchers on a lonely road in the Mississippi countryside. It was terribly hot and flat. There were only about 100 of us walking. A police car rode along behind because a lot of people in Mississippi were angry at Dr. King and felt he was just a trouble-maker. They were ready to make trouble themselves because they didn't want to see his friends vote. A big truck crawled up ahead filled with dozens of reporters and photographers. It surprised me that even though there were just a few of us, the whole world seemed to be interested in Dr. King's journey. I didn't realize that by the end of the march our little band would grow to fifty-thousand strong to hear Martin Luther King speak in front of the state capital in Jackson, Mississippi.

The sun beat down on the pavement making the heat almost unbearable to me as the road guided us through tree plantations, farms, and swamps. My white skin began to turn lobster red. Someone gave me a hat, and I made sure I wore a shirt with long sleeves. Occasionally we would pass a stream and I would wade in, soaking my sneakers and socks to the skin, only to find them bone dry again a half hour later.

I liked to walk with the old folks from Dr. King's church. They would tell me, "It's just wonderful that you white folks have come from so far away to help us register voters."
Our little band also included urgent young people who talked about something called "Black Power". They were very impatient to set right the wrongs that had been done to blacks. And there were men with scowls on their faces who rarely spoke and always wore overalls and t-shirts. They kept to the outside of the

group, and you could see a few walking beside the police car. They always walked with Dr. King. People called them, "the protectors."

Whenever we approached a town, we would detour around the rich neighbourhoods and walk through the shanty streets, where people would greet us and join the march. Our numbers sometimes grew to several hundred. People left their garden hoses running so we could drink and soak our sweaty shirts. Smiling neighbours lined the sidewalks and front porches, and some donated coins to a collection hat. I handed out leaflets explaining how important it was to vote.

As we left town our numbers would dwindle again, although by the end of each day there were more of us than the day before.

We spent the nights in sleeping bags under the stars. The men in overalls did not sleep, but patrolled the outside of our camp. The day before I had arrived the march had been attacked by angry men. So, for some of us, the nights were a nervous time. Yet I remember a lovely evening at the university in Tupalo, where we were fed chicken and given showers. That night we felt very safe sleeping on the grassy square in the centre of the black university.

I have many memories to share about my adventure, but the most important event occurred when we reached the city of Jackson, where Martin Luther King was to speak.

Jackson, the capital of Mississippi, marked the end of our march. Approaching the city our numbers really began to swell. About a thousand of us entered the outskirts and wound our way through the slums toward the capital building. The sidewalks were packed with people who had been waiting for us, and they stepped into the street to join the procession. There was cheering and waving as the excitement and numbers mounted. Neighbours would reach out their hands and we would hold on, sweeping them into the march with our magnetism.

"Join us," we would call. "Come to the city hall."

I saw an old woman with white hair and a wrinkled face standing on her front porch, laughing and shouting our praises as if we were the Great Emancipator himself.

"Come on," I shouted. "Martin Luther King is going to speak."

The joy inside her bubbled over and, reaching out, she stepped with us into the street. My friends and I embraced her and we marched together for a few paces.

"NO!" someone shouted. "Leave her alone."

A younger woman, probably her daughter, pushed through the crowd to reclaim her mother's hand.

"You don't know what you're going to find at city hall." The woman's face was distressed and frightened. "You don't know what you're leading her into. Leave this old woman alone." Firmly she guided her mother back to the porch.

Our numbers grew and grew, and soon the streets were so filled that I could see no end to the line in either direction. I felt like I was part of an army leading the wave of the future. Yes, I recognized fear in some of the faces we passed, but I was not afraid. We were invincible.

We walked for such a long time that I became grateful to have left the old woman behind because she surely would have become tired. But we forged on, shouting and chanting, toward the city hall where Martin Luther King would speak. There were thousands upon thousands of us now, marching loudly in the spirit of this momentous occasion.

As the city hall drew near, the chanting up ahead died down, and by the time I reached the park that circled the capital building, there was utter silence.

Then I saw them... angry men everywhere! On the steps of the building stood a line of angry men with sticks and weapons. In front of them was another ring of men with helmets and bigger weapons. And a hundred yards closer, only paces from us, a third line of men surrounded us.

Despite our numbers, my fear began to rise. I stood near the edge of the crowd, not very far from one of these men. His face was blank as if he didn't see the huge assembly that filled the park. He didn't seem angry or mean. I think this particular young man was as scared as me, because if fighting broke out we would all be in trouble, including him. Standing almost shoulder to shoulder with him was one of "the protectors," in overalls and a t-shirt. He was smiling, but it was not a friendly smile. It was a leer, the way a wolf shows his teeth. Looking along this third line, I saw a "protector" standing side by side with almost every one of the angry men. But I did not feel protected. I was very frightened.

We were pressed so close together in the afternoon heat that I found it hard to breath. Or was it the silence of the crowd that had become overpowering? I could not tell if it was a silence borne of fear or of strength. Perhaps it was a silence of respect as the multitude awaited its leader.

But as for me, I was silent because I was scared. You could have shovelled me into a bucket I was so scared. Someone was crying. Was it me? no.... OH NO! There, a few feet behind me was the old woman! Obviously her daughter's warning had not been heeded, and we had led her miles from her home into the lion's jaws. She stood still and straight, not looking at the angry lines or the capital building, but fixed her eyes on the podium a hundred yards away where Martin Luther King was to make his address. But she could not keep the tears from her eyes, nor an occasional whimper of fear from her throat. I felt terribly responsible. Her daughter was right. What would happen to her if the angry men charged? How could we protect her from the blows?

It seemed like an eternity before Martin Luther King stepped up to the podium. He began with the words, "I have a dream." And in his dream he painted a beautiful picture of the goal that awaited us at the end of our struggle. He spoke for a long time and finished with the words, "I still have a dream." Many of us were crying when he stepped down. My knees felt weak. Dr. King's speech made me feel like a tiny drop in a gigantic bucket of humanity that someday would spill over and wash a cool wave of justice and freedom across the hot land. There was a terrible lump in my throat, and I knew that if I spoke my glistening eyes would overflow with tears.

After a silent moment, a voice sang out from somewhere in the crowd.
"*I'm gonna lay down my sword and shield,*" and some people answered,
"*Down by the riverside.*" A thousand took up the song,
"*Down by the riverside.*" And then fifty thousand voices were singing,
"*Down by the riverside.*
I'm gonna lay down my sword and shield,
Down by the riverside.
I'm gonna study war no more."
Suddenly a voice with the strength of Joshua leaped into counterpoint from behind me.
"*Oh lord I'm gonna...*"
And the congregation answered: "*Study war no more*"
"*Oh lord, I'm gonna,*" ..."*Study war no...*"
"*Study war no more.*"
It was the old woman! The song surged through her like an electric charge, and before the verse ended her fear was conquered and the reassuring power of her voice covered us with a blanket of strength and peace. It lifted our spirits and made us one. It seemed like all fifty thousand of us could hear her voice, if that were possible. And she guided us through the song like the lead singer in a

church choir. The music in her soul must have reached a hundred ears in both directions. I know that the angry men heard it, and so did the man with the wolf smile. And the power of her voice filled me with a spirit that banished the lump in my throat and gave me back my own voice so that I too could join the choir.

"*I'm gonna study war no more.*"

OTHER BOOKS OF INTEREST

The Dulcimer Book by Jean Ritchie. (Oak Publications, A Division of Embassy Music Corporation, 33 West 60th St., New York, N.Y. 10023)

Folk Instruments, Make Them and Play Them, It's Easy and It's Fun by Dennis Waring. (Hyperion Press Limited, 300 Wales Avenue, Winnipeg, Manitoba. R2M 2S9)

Homegrown Music by Marc Bristol. (Madrona Publishers, Inc., 2116 Western Avenue, Seattle, Washington 98121)

Homemade Instruments by Dallas Cline. (Oak Publications, A Division of Embassy Music Corporation, 33 West 60th St., New York, N.Y. 10023)

Homemade Musical Instruments by Tom Keynton. (Drake Publishers, Inc., 381 Park Avenue South, New York, N.Y. 10016)

How to Play Nearly Everything by Dallas Cline. (Oak Publications, A Division of Embassy Music Corporation, 33 West 60th St., New York, N.Y. 10023)

Simple Folk Instruments to Make and to Play by Ilene Hunter and Marilyn Judson. (Simon and Schuster, A Division of Gulf and Western Corporation, Simon and Schuster Building, Rockefeller Center, 1230 Avenue of the Americas, New York, N.Y. 10020)

What to Do Until the Music Teacher Comes by Louise Glatt. (Berandol Music Limited, 11 St. Joseph St., Toronto, Ontario. M4Y 1J8)

Musical Instruments of the Southern Appalachian Mountains by John Rice Irwin. (Schiffer Publishing Ltd., 1979, Box E, Exton, Pennsylvania)